The Last Maopo

The Last Maopo

The Life and First World War Sacrifice of Wiremu Maopo

Letters from the First World War
by Wiremu Tanai Kaihau Maopo
(1886–1929)

Narrative by his great-granddaughter
Tania Te Rangingangana Simpson
(1965–)

He tūhononga ā nuku, he tūhononga ā rangi;
Ka tika ko te hono.

A uniting from below, a uniting from above;
The bond is everlasting.

Ka tāpea tēnei pukapuka ki tōku tupuna ki a Wiremu Maopo me āna mokopuna, rātou ko āku tamariki, ki a Ariāhuia rāua ko Hawaiki.

This book is dedicated to Wiremu Maopo and his great-great-grandchildren, including my children Ariāhuia and Hawaiki Te Ruki. From my whakapapa they are Tainui, Ngāpuhi and Ngāi Tahu. This is their Ngāi Tahu story.

Published by Libro International, an imprint of Oratia Media Ltd, 783 West Coast Road, Oratia, Auckland 0604, New Zealand (www.librointernational.com).

Copyright © 2014 Tania Te Rangingangana Simpson

The copyright holder assert her moral rights in the work.

This book is copyright. Except for the purposes of fair reviewing, no part of this publication may be reproduced or transmitted in any form or by any means, whether electronic, digital or mechanical, including photocopying, recording, any digital or computerised format, or any information storage and retrieval system, including by any means via the Internet, without permission in writing from the publisher. Infringers of copyright render themselves liable to prosecution.

ISBN 978-1-877514-66-1
Ebook ISBN 978-1-877514-67-8

Edited by Carolyn Lagahetau
Designed by Cheryl Smith, Macarn Design

Front cover: Wiremu Maopo (see p. 134); Māori soldiers perform a haka (p. 120)
Back cover: Marjorie Joyce and Phoebe (p. 141); Māori soldiers in the trenches (p. 80)

First published 2014
Printed in China by Nordica

Contents

1	Reconnecting	9
2	The early Maopo whānau	15
3	Wiremu Kaihau Maopo meets Phoebe Prentice	22
4	Wiremu goes to war	27
5	Phoebe goes to the Bethany Home	38
6	Phoebe's baby	46
7	A world at war	55
8	Phoebe: moving on	63
9	Letters from home	76
10	Wiremu visits 'Blighty'	83
11	Changes at home	91
12	The onset of winter	108
13	Military hospital	124
14	Wiremu returns home	128
15	Life after war	138
16	Finding Marjorie Joyce	140
17	Whakapapa Ngāi Tahu	143
18	Maopo whakapapa	146

Acknowledgements ... 147
Author's note ... 149
Events in Wiremu's life ... 151
Notes ... 155

1

Reconnecting

The much-referenced Māori proverb 'E kore te kūmara e kōrero ana mō tōna ake nei reka!' — 'The kūmara never speaks of its own sweetness' — is a fundamental Māori tenet and is a philosophical underpinning of this story. This is a personal story that is shared not to emphasise our tūpuna or whānau, but to provide insight into society, community and life in Aotearoa during the First World War. It is with some reticence that the personal aspects of the story are included to provide context and completeness. The story begins with my own involvement with the subject of this book.

Throughout our childhood my maternal cousins and I knew that part of our Māori heritage came through our grandmother Marjorie Joyce, though she would never speak about it.

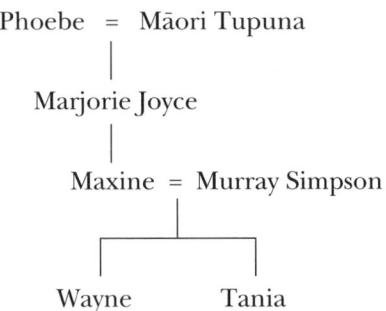

Whakapapa Chart 1

❦ The Last *Maopo*

My Pākehā father taught my brother and me basic phrases in te Reo Māori, which he had learned growing up at Hangatiki in the King Country. He raised us to enjoy muttonbirds, hāngi and boil-up and to appreciate Māori culture. He was determined that we should retain and be proud of our Māori identity. Being raised within Ngāti Maniapoto, an affinity to Māori culture was a feature of my childhood. Many of our family had married into Māori whānau and I considered them all my relations.

When we were young my father broached the subject of our heritage with his mother-in-law, Nanna Joyce. It was a tapu subject that the family did not speak of. However, late one night he noticed a light on in the house and, as she was sitting up by herself, he privately asked Nanna if she would explain her Māori heritage to my mother, so in time she could let my brother and I know our whakapapa. Nanna replied that she was unaware of the details of her ancestry. Later, she instructed my mother to make sure my father never raised the matter with her again.

When I was 12 years old Nanna Joyce's maternal half-sisters, Betty and Bonny, came to visit. During their visit I learned that Nanna was adopted. Our family gave confusing responses to questions about Nanna's heritage. My mother told me she thought Nanna was Hawai'ian. Later in life I discovered that many of the kaumātua in the Otorohanga district thought my grandmother was from the Pacific Islands. They had assumed this because she entertained them at parties with her island-style dancing.

I met Nanna Joyce's Pākehā birth mother for the first and only time when I was 13 years old. I caught a ride from Te Kuiti with our boarder and went to visit Great Nanna Phoebe, who lived in Palmerston North. I climbed the steps of her house with some trepidation, carrying baking and preserves from my mother. Great Nanna Phoebe opened the door and it seemed like she only came up to my chest; the conditions of age had shrunk her frame. The delight of having a mokopuna visit showed on her face.

She showed me her home and over a cup of tea we talked about her parents and their life in Palmerston North. Her father was a

Reconnecting

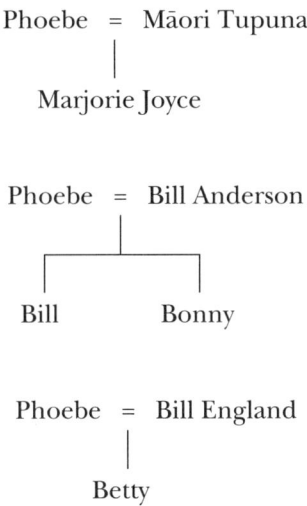

Whakapapa Chart 2

brickmaker, having been apprenticed to her grandfather. His brick mill had made the red bricks for the All Saints Anglican Church in The Square, Palmerston North in 1914 and she told me there were 365,000 bricks. As she talked I hoped that she would tell me about Nanna's Māori father, but she never brought it up. Still influenced by Nanna's tapu on the subject, I did not ask her about it.

She gave me preserves to take home to my mother and, as it was bitterly cold and I was not warmly dressed, she insisted on giving me a warm coat. She opened a dark wooden chest and pulled out a beautiful brown coat with gold buttons, in perfect condition. The sleeves came just past my elbows and it fell to mid-thigh, about which she was apologetic, but I told her that was the fashion and it would be great. I left with all my questions unanswered but with the joy of having had time with my tupuna. I never saw her again.

The strong pull of whakapapa was a constant feature in my life. It was neither merely a choice, nor an interest. It was a calling, a constant voice. At age 19 I summoned the courage to ask Nanna Joyce about our heritage. She was unhappy about my raising the subject. After I posed the question the room fell silent and heavy. 'Why do you want to know?' she said without looking at me. I tried to explain my need to know our identity, our heritage, our whenua, but my words failed to move her. 'I don't know,' she responded without looking at me. There was a long period of awkward silence. She was clearly upset with me. Nevertheless I persevered, as this was likely to be my only shot at ever raising the subject with her. 'Do you know your father's name?' I asked. 'No,' she responded, and lifted the remote control to turn the television on, raising the volume loud, a clear sign that the conversation was over. I sat for a while and tried to watch TV and make small talk with her, hoping to lift the heavy atmosphere in the room, but it only seemed to get worse, so I thought it best to leave. By the time I arrived back at my mother's house, a few minutes down the road, Nanna had phoned my mother and instructed her to ensure that I never raised the matter again.

Out of respect for my grandmother I tried to leave things alone, but the problem was, the issue wouldn't leave me alone. My questions reappeared at every turn. After a period of months I decided to continue investigating, without Nanna's knowledge. This was going against her wishes, but I considered knowing our identity and whakapapa was our birthright. I told my mother of my intention. I knew it would be hard for my mother to go against Nanna's wishes. She had to choose between respecting her mother's wishes and supporting her daughter. I always appreciated that she chose to support me.

Over a period of years I spoke to family members and old friends of Nanna's to see if anyone could give me any clue or hint as to the identity of Nanna's father. Most of the people I spoke with didn't know, but Nanna's half-sister, my Great-Aunty Betty, had some information. Phoebe, their shared mother, had told Aunty Betty about Nanna's father and Aunty Betty passed on to me what she could remember of their conversation. Nanna Joyce's father was Māori and came from the South Island, somewhere near Leeston. Phoebe had lived there for a time with her elder sister, Emma, and drove the farm cream-cart to the creamery. Nanna's father fought and died in the First World War. His name was Bill and he had a Māori surname but she couldn't remember what it was. Bill had written to Great-Nanna Phoebe but her family had intercepted and burned the letters without her knowledge. Phoebe had not learned of this until many years later, after her parents were dead. At last, I had found the beginning of a pathway towards unravelling the question of our heritage.

I scanned the war records for soldiers with the name Bill, William or Wiremu who were from the South Island. I searched the National Archives and the National Library and I read books on the First World War, but without a surname I couldn't make a clear and definite connection. At every dead end I would give up searching, putting it aside for months or years, but inevitably the pull would return and I would start looking again. After seemingly exhausting my options, in 2002 I gave it one final attempt. I placed a letter in the local Leeston paper. To my surprise I received a response from the Taumutu Rūnanga, which provided a key to revealing our whakapapa.

> The dairy factory that Phoebe took the milk to, we understand to be 'Lakeside Dairy Factory'. A member of our Rūnanga believes that the identity of the man known locally as 'Bill' is Tane (Tani) Maopo ...[1]

I now had a possible surname: Maopo. I was optimistic that this could be our tupuna. Phoebe's grandmother was named Harriet Hill, initials H.H. Phoebe was Phoebe Prentice, initials P.P. I had guessed that in keeping with this tradition, Marjorie Joyce's surname would start with an 'M', to give initials M.M. Marjorie Maopo would fit with the family pattern.

Shortly after this discovery, I received a letter from Richard Manning that provided more information about Wiremu Tanai Maopo. Richard's family were related to Mop Te Morokiekie Manning, who was a whāngai son to Wiremu. Wiremu believed he had no children of his own, so he arranged a whāngai son from his wider whānau to inherit the whānau land. Wiremu's whāngai, Mop, had no children, and he in turn passed the land interests to his sister, Waiwehi, who later distributed the interests among the Manning whānau. This was Richard's whānau.

❧ The Last *Maopo*

(Bill) Wiremu Tanai Kaihau Maopo
|
Te Morokiekie (Mop) Manning – *(Whāngai)*

Whakapapa Chart 3

Nanna Joyce had passed on by the time we learned the identity of her father. As the eldest living descendant, my mother travelled to Christchurch to meet with Richard Manning. She took with her a photo of Nanna Joyce and Great Nanna Phoebe and Richard gave us a photo of Wiremu. The connection had been made and the story unfolded, providing more evidence and proof of Wiremu and Phoebe's connection.

    This is their story.

2

The early Maopo whānau

On the eastern side of the South Island of New Zealand, a narrow shingle spit separates the large and shallow Lake Waihora from the rolling sea. On the banks of Lake Waihora a Māori community has lived for more than 600 years at the place they named Taumutu, at the southern end of Kaitōrete Spit.

Te Waipounamu, known for the majestic beauty of its mountains, lakes, fiords and coastline, can be a cold and bleak place in winter, especially when living in a small hut in a windy coastal village. Over the generations Ngāti Moki people developed resilience and a rhythm with the changing cycles of the natural environment. They fished the lake and the sea, and opened the sand spit to drain and clear the lake and release tuna (eels) for migration into the ocean. They did this by dragging harakeke stalks through the shingle to dig out a narrow channel, then letting the water do the rest of the work, scouring the channel wider and wider as it passed through.

The roaring ocean provided a bounty of seafood, and playful dolphins were a regular sight along the shores. Lake Waihora, with its swamplands, clear water tributaries and springs, was a food store of tuna, pātiki (flounder), aua (yellow-eyed mullet), kanakana (lamprey), inanga (whitebait), pipi and a variety of birds such as pūtakitaki (paradise shelduck).

This food store, along with the South Island's southernmost supply

❦ The Last *Maopo*

of kūmara stores, made Ngāti Moki an important trading partner for inland tribes. Taumutu was a major centre for working and trading of pounamu, with nearby access across the Canterbury Plains and over the alpine passes of the Southern Alps to the West Coast.[1] After the Treaty of Waitangi was signed in 1840, there was a progressive increase in settler, government and missionary activity throughout Aotearoa, which gradually extended into the most remote locations. Surveyors were eventually sent to Taumutu to survey the lands as a basis from which to create deeds of title for trading and settlement.[2]

Pioneer surveyors Thomas Cass and Charles Torlesse arrived in Taumutu on 1 March 1849. They camped at a new Māori hut belonging to the Maopo whānau, on the sand hills within Taumutu Pā. The pā included a row of whānau huts in a one-sided street.[3] The 1844 census records 20 people of Ngāti Ruahikihiki and Ngāi Tūahuriri living at Taumutu under the chieftainship of Tiakikai and Maopo.[4] The surveyors were given paradise shelduck to eat, provided by the Maopo whānau, and three grey ducks that they had shot themselves. They stayed a few days undertaking their work, and they paid Mrs Maopo four shillings for potatoes, paradise shelducks, slings and lodgings.[5] Mrs Maopo's house, courtyard and gardens were well kept and visitors were well taken care of.[6]

Te Maiharanui Atarea Maopo was a 13-year-old boy when the pioneer surveyors came to stay with his parents, Kawana Te Wakaihau Maopo and Wera Mōkihi. His siblings were Tohu Kawana, Riria and Kurariwai. Te Maiharanui was named after the ūpoko ariki of Akaroa, who had been taken captive by Te Rauparaha. Te Maiharanui had died a few years before the birth of his namesake.

Te Maiharanui's father, Kawana Maopo, was a signatory to the infamous Kemp's Purchase, signed on the HMS *Fly* at Akaroa on 12 June 1848. He was a Trustee of the Native Reserve established at Taumutu in 1868. He was known to have had two wives, Wera and Ngarara, in the late 1850s, and in 1866, at an estimated age of 78 years,[7] was still an active leader.

After the death of his parents, Te Maiharanui Maopo inherited the family lands at Taumutu, Maitahi and Waipopo. He married Ani Wira from Wairewa, a village located at the other end of the lake. Ani's

The early Maopo whānau

Te Wakaihai Maopo = Pii Te Raki
|
Kawana = Te Wera Mokihi
|
Atarea Ta Maiharanui Maopo = Ani Wera
|
Wiremu Kaihau Maopo = Phoebe Prentice

Whakapapa Chart 4

tūpuna lands were at Arowhenua, Taumutu, Wairewa, Raukapuka, Onuku, Kapuratiki, Kaiapoi and Kapumātiki. Te Maiharanui and Ani were married at Temuka and settled at Taumutu, raising a family of 13 children. They looked after their lands and leased some to settlers. Records show that in 1889 John Patterson leased 5.3 hectares of land from Te Maiharanui Maopo. There were similar arrangements with various other Pākehā settlers.

The Taiaroa whānau was another well known family in the area. In the late 1870s the Honourable Hori Kerei Taiaroa, Member of Parliament for Southern Māori, moved with his family from Otakou to Taumutu as he had family land there and it was closer to Wellington. Te Maiharanui Maopo and others assisted with the building of the Taiaroa whare, Awhitu House, which became a centre of influence and politics for Māori, and continued to play an important role for South Island Māori during the 20th century.[8]

Christianity was a big part of Maopo family life. Charles Creed, a pioneer Wesleyan missionary, had visited Taumutu in October 1845, when Te Maiharanui was nine years old. Over time Te Maiharanui became active in local church activities and eventually he became a lay preacher. He led services at Taumutu Pā on a regular basis and was the Taumutu elected member to the Māori Council. Te Maiharanui was regarded by many as 'the most honest man in the country'.[9] Like many Māori of this time, he was well versed in the spiritual traditions of his ancestors, and he balanced this with the spiritual teachings of the Christian faith.

17

❦ The Last *Maopo*

When Te Maiharanui was 49 years old he assisted Hori Kerei Taiaroa with the building of the Hone Wetere Church at Taumutu Pā. The church was officially opened in 1885. Two services were held on the opening day and a document was read out to the congregation, gifting the church and land to the Methodist Conference of New Zealand.

The gift of the church was formalised in a written agreement. Te Maiharanui and three other chiefs of the district signed the document on behalf of the local people and, in accordance with Māori protocol, the document was placed in a bottle and laid in stone under the floor of the church.[10] Te Maiharanui continued to function as a lay preacher at the church for the next 30 years.[11]

Wiremu Kaihau Tanai Maopo was born in March 1886. His siblings included Kakoho Amiria, Karoko, Kataraina, Hone, Rutu, Te Morokiekie, Kihau, Henare Maka To Kapi, Taare Te Kopipiti, Rawinia Hinewai, Eruera Noho Kotahi and Rara.

In 1883, Sedgemere School was opened. It was the first school to which Māori children were admitted on an equal footing with Europeans, and it existed as a distinct entity from the Māori Native Schools.[12] School photos and the school roll from the period show the Maopo children attended Sedgemere School. At the time it was common to assign Pākehā names to Māori children when they attended school, and the Maopo children were no exception. The school photos and the roll show their names as Eliza, Moloney, John, Amelia, William, Henry and Charles.[13] Rawinia seems to have broken with school tradition and her name is recorded on the roll as Rawene. The family surname was challenging for English speakers, as it is frequently recorded in the school roll and in public notices as Moap or Moapo. Their father, Atarea Te Maiharanui Maopo, was also known as Andrew.

Despite being raised within a big family and in a good community, Wiremu's childhood was marred with sadness. Māori families suffered greatly from a lack of resistance to the new viruses and diseases that were carried by the English settlers. Tuberculosis and influenza found their way into the Maopo family and one by one the Maopo children succumbed. Kakaho Amiria died when Wiremu was 13; Rutu died when Wiremu was 16; Te Morokiekie died when Wiremu was 21; Kihau

The Māori Church at Taumutu, with members of the Māori and European congregation. Christchurch City Libraries, *The Weekly Press*, 19 July 1899, p. 51

died when Wiremu was 24; and brother Henare died at the age of 24, when Wiremu was 27. The entire village mourned the family deaths. Henare's funeral was reported in the local newspaper:

> *Last Thursday there was carried to his last resting place in the little Pah cemetery the body of Henare Moapo (Harry Moap). His death, just on the verge of manhood, and comparatively sudden, cast a*

> gloom over the Pah and surrounding district. The deceased was popular with both Pakeha and Maori, was a keen footballer and always ready to take his part in any social gathering.
>
> Nearly every house in the vicinity sent its representative, so that, with Maori friends and relatives from other Pahs, there was a good gathering at the church. Here a short service, conducted by the Rev. T.A. Joughin was held. At the graveside prayers in the Maori language were offered by the Rev. Joughin and Mr Andrew Aterea Moapo. A special hymn, sung in Maori was very impressive.
>
> Mr Aterea Moapo, who is a local preacher at the Maori church, has been an inhabitant of the Pah for many years. Out of a large family he now has only three living. Much sympathy is felt both for Mr Moapo and his wife.
>
> Ellesmere Guardian, *30 April 1913*

The long list of family bereavements was not yet over. Wiremu's mother, Ani, died shortly after Henare, further compounding the family's grief. She was aged 60.[14]

> With but a few weeks interval another grave was opened at the pah cemetery and the body of Mrs Moapo was laid beside that of her son. Again a goodly gathering of Pakeha and Maori assembled to show their respect and sympathy with Mr Aterea Moapo and his family. The funeral service was conducted by the Rev. H.G Hawkins and Miss Hapley acted as organist while a hymn was sung. At the conclusion of the service at the graveside the usual Maori burial chant was sung, the soft splash of the waves a few yards distant seeming to act as a fitting accompaniment. Upon the coffin were placed the private mats of the deceased to be buried with her in her last long sleep.
>
> Mrs Moapo had been blind for some time, but managed with wonderful exactitude to weave colours and patterns into her native handwork. She suffered from heart trouble, and the shock of her son's death hastened her end. Out of a large family of thirteen, three only now survive.
>
> Ellesmere Guardian, *25 June 1913*

The early Maopo whānau

'Funeral of the Late Mr Hapa Taiaroa, The Ceremony at the Grave, Reverend JP Cocks officiating.'
Christchurch City Libraries, *The Canterbury Times*, 23 August 1905

Wiremu and Taare (Charles), Wiremu's only remaining brother, were keen footballers and both played in the Southbridge team. Sadly, at 19 years old, in October 1914, Taare died, a year after Harry and when Wiremu was 28. In the space of a few short years Wiremu, his sister Hinewai and his father, Te Maiharanui, were the only survivors of the once large Maopo family, their lives scarred by the grief of the overwhelming loss of a wife and mother and a large family of children.

3

Wiremu Kaihau Maopo meets Phoebe Prentice

After the death of his mother, Wiremu occasionally worked picking potatoes in the Lakeside and Sedgemere districts, but for the most part he worked as a farmhand for the Fincham family on their family farm, Willow Glen. The Fincham farm was a short walk from the Maopo whare, which was near Ngāti Moki Pā.

The families in the area knew each other well. Wiremu, Henry Pohio 'Daddy', Fred Stretz and Len Cant were among those who worked for the Finchams at Willow Glen. The boys often joined the Fincham family for meals during the harvest, where Granny Fincham would take them under her wing and good-humouredly chastise them for any misbehaviour. She would especially growl at Wiremu for 'cackling' at the table. He in turn would give Granny plenty of cheek to keep her firing.

Granny Fincham was a widow. She had settled at Willow Glen farm with her husband Thomas in 1864. Her youngest son, Herb, was 'the boss'. Willow Glen was the gathering place for church services, it served as the local post office, and the barn was used for district dances and social gatherings until Sedgemere Hall was built in 1916.[1] Herb Fincham was the president of the Leeston Show, which was a great local annual event.

Virginie (Virgie) Fincham, Granny's granddaughter, also lived at Willow Glen. Her mother had died when she was young. Virgie ran the house and the post office on the farm. Emily Cant was also part of the Willow Glen household, and Jessie Lochhead was a close friend of the girls. It was a bustling household and there were many happy occasions there.[2]

Jessie Lochhead, Emily Cant, Virgie Fincham.
Photograph supplied by Joan Overhill

❧ The Last *Maopo*

Wiremu passed the Schnelle Farm each day on his way to work at Willow Glen. Fred, the Schnelles' son, had gone to the North Island to work on a farm in the Manawatu. While there he met and married Emma Prentice, and in 1898 they moved back to Taumutu with their young daughter Mildred, to take over the family farm.[3] Emma did not adjust easily to life in the small rural South Island community, and she missed her family and friends in the North Island. Fred decided to send for Emma's younger sister Phoebe to come and live with them, in the hope that having her sister with her would help Emma to settle. Phoebe would help Emma with the house, the children and the farm work.

Phoebe absolutely loved her new life. The two young women were from a family of 13 children, daughters of a Salvation Army captain from Palmerston North. They had a very strict and righteous upbringing. As the youngest of the children, Phoebe relished the adventure and freedom of leaving home, and she welcomed the Taumutu way of life, becoming a regular at community activities, church services and local dances. However, having her sister with her was a small consolation for Emma, who still struggled to settle.

The wedding of Fred Gulliver and Margaret Patterson at the Schnelle homestead, 1908.
Photograph supplied by Roger Gilbert

It didn't take long for Wiremu to learn about the interesting newcomer and to subsequently make her acquaintance. Wiremu lived with his father, Te Maiharanui, and his sister, Hinewai, in the house next door to Fred and Emma Schnelle's farm. This was not far from the Fincham farm where Wiremu worked, and there were plenty of opportunities for socialising.

Before long Phoebe and Wiremu were courting, taking long walks across the farm and along the beach, Phoebe's young niece Milly in tow as an unofficial chaperone. Wiremu would sometimes accompany Phoebe when she drove the cream-cart to the Lakeside creamery, or meet up with her along the way. Some evenings, after lights out, he would climb stealthily through Phoebe's bedroom window and over Milly's bed to visit Phoebe, without raising any of the senior occupants of the house. Older sister Emma would most definitely have disapproved and young Milly was instructed to keep quiet about it.

Phoebe and Wiremu knew their relationship was controversial. In many quarters, interracial marriages were not yet socially accepted. Wiremu's sister Hinewai had encountered strong opposition when she and Len Cant announced their plans to marry. Len's family sent him off to the North Island where he worked on the Maraekakaho run out of Hastings. He returned after seven years, undaunted and determined to marry Hinewai. After they married Len was disinherited by his family.[4]

The First World War began in August 1914 and New Zealand pledged its support for Britain. Enlisting in the war was voluntary, but Māori political leaders paved the way and encouraged young Māori to participate by volunteering for a separate Māori Contingent. Wiremu had served with the Ellesmere Mounted Rifles and when the call came for South Island Māori men to join the fighting forces, he enlisted with the 2nd Māori Contingent of what was to become the Māori Pioneer Battalion.

Phoebe was naturally upset by the news, but this was a time when many families saw their men depart, not knowing if they would return. Enlistment was recognised as a national duty and Wiremu was proud to fight on behalf of friends and family at Taumutu. He and Phoebe could always resume their relationship after the war. They both knew there was the risk that he might not come home from the battlefields.

The Taumutu region with locations relevant to the Maopo whānau.
Map supplied by Peter Caldwell

4

Wiremu goes to war

In February 1915 the 1st Māori Contingent sailed from Wellington to Egypt. Known as Te Hokowhitu a Tū, the Contingent paved the way for Māori soldiers to represent their nation in the First World War. When their troopship steamed into Mudros Harbour, they passed British warships on each side. 'Who are you?' the British sailors shouted from the rails of their ships. 'The Maoris!' was the reply. 'Oh, the Maoris? Three cheers for the Maoris!', the British sailors shouted, breaking out their hip-hip-hoorays.[1] Their arrival in Egypt was similarly heralded by loud cheering from their Pākehā counterparts,[2] who were more than pleased to see them.

The Māori Contingent was intended to work as a labour force, but their proximity to the battlefields meant they were vulnerable to injury from bombs and bullets. One Māori soldier was shot in his sleep and, being either exhausted or a sound sleeper, he did not rouse and awoke later from the cold and found himself lying in a pool of blood from a flesh wound.[3]

The 1st Māori Contingent soon found themselves embroiled in the battles of Gallipoli and a second Māori Contingent was recruited in New Zealand to provide reinforcement. Wiremu stepped forward to join the second intake.

Shortly after announcing he was enlisting, Wiremu was saying his goodbyes with no time to organise a proper farewell. He departed for training camp at the end of June 1915. He was aged 29 years.

During his time away Wiremu wrote regularly to his family and friends in Taumutu. Among correspondence to family members, Wiremu and the other soldiers who had worked at Willow Glen also wrote to Granny Fincham to keep her advised of their progress. Virgie Fincham responded to the letters on her grandmother's behalf and subsequently the soldiers became regular correspondents with Virgie. She kept the letters they sent her, and it is through her collection of letters that we are able to retrace Wiremu's experiences as he recounts them.

>(Please address all letters to Private W.K. Maopo
>As my name is in Maori)
>Fort Takapuna
>Maori Camp
>July 6th 1915
>
>Miss Virgie Fincham
>Taumutu Leeston
>
>Dear Virgie
>Just to inform you all that I have arrived at the Maori Reinforcement camp quite safe although I was very ill with sea sickness coming across in the boat. There are about four hundred men in camp at present, another hundred expected next week. I might mention there are some wild looking customers of Maoris up here and some can't speak a word of English. As I have not much time at present I may mention before I conclude that if you don't mind to address all my letters to Maori Reinforcement's Fort Takapuna Devonport.
>Remember me to all at home. Tell old Tom I wish to be remembered to him and that I will write to him later on as the bugle is sounding to fall in for parade. I will now close with wishes and Arohanui
>
>Yours sincerely
>Friend Bill

Shortly after Wiremu's departure, Phoebe discovered she was pregnant. Naturally this was a shock, and with Wiremu away she had few options available to her. She reluctantly confided in her elder sister Emma, who immediately informed their parents in Palmerston North of Phoebe's condition. The news of Phoebe's pregnancy was scandalous for her highly moral, religious father and mother, and they made a plan to ensure that the matter would be dealt with quietly so that no one would ever know and Phoebe would be free to find a good husband.

Marriage to Wiremu was out of the question. Wiremu had gone off to war, making marriage impossible, and even if he was at home a mixed-race marriage was unacceptable. Even more unacceptable was a pregnancy out of wedlock. Phoebe was left alone to deal with her pregnancy and her forceful, disapproving parents.

Wiremu wrote to Phoebe but received no reply. He was perplexed and presumed she had lost interest in him. He had no knowledge of her situation. He continued to write to her but none of his letters reached her. Many years later, after the death of her parents, Phoebe's sister Nell confessed to having destroyed the letters as they arrived, under strict instruction from their parents, who were determined to prevent any relationship. Wiremu continued to write to other family and friends, including his good friend Virgie Fincham.

Fort Takapuna
July 22nd 1915

Dear Virgie
Your most welcome letter to hand today. And I was very pleased to hear from you. I really thought that you had forgotten to answer my note. I am keeping first rate hoping this will find you all well at Willow Glen. How's all the Show horses, I suppose all the boys are busy feeding them. I heard from Mrs Cant that Sandy has returned. How's the boy keeping? I don't think that Phoebe is troubling about me.
Last Saturday all the boys were given general leave to go to Auckland from 3.30 until 11 p.m., a lot of them got beastly drunk and were detained in Auckland until the next day. I must say we

are all a very happy lot of fellows in Camp. Of course things will be better when the huts are completed. There's a big hall to be built also for dancing, a billiard Saloon and a skating rink, we also have a piano sent to us from Wellington.

Dear Virgie, I am expecting to be on general leave for home in six weeks' time, providing I am a good boy, several of the boys have already deserted camp so if any more of the boys break camp, general leave will not be granted to anyone.

Last Sunday afternoon a massed Band parade was held on the Takapuna Racecourse opposite our Camp in aid of the Wounded boys from the front, practically the whole camp were there besides people from the surrounding districts, about twenty bands paraded and about four or five hundred pounds was collected, not bad was it.

Next Wednesday a Football Match between our Company, that is the Bs, and the Royal Artillery, will be played to raise funds to form a brass band for the Maori Contingent. The whole Camp has already subscribed £35 towards the band.

Dear Virgie. I wish you would send me up the buster so that I may know how things are going on at dear old Ellesmere. I wish you will also send me up Emily's address for I have forgotten her address. I am getting along fine with my drill and am going up for a signalling exam, the first week in August, exams are held every Month for different positions.

I have had a letter from George Lochhead informing me that they are removing from the old place shortly. I think you will all miss the Lochheads, especially the Boss, tell him so from me will you. Is Burkett back yet? Well Virgie, I think I have told you all for the present, so will now conclude, with my best love to all at Willow Glen, not forgetting your dear self. I will now bid you Goodbye, and Arohanui.

From,
Yours sincerely
Bill

In early August, soldiers of the 1st Māori Contingent fought at Gallipoli alongside their Pākehā countrymen, suffering heavy losses. The Māori Contingent quickly earned the respect of their compatriots. Major Buck wrote in his diary of his pride in hearing the Māori haka, which signalled a successful advance: 'Rattle of musketry, then silence, and the loud English cheer, followed by a Māori haka. Owing to the Māoris being distributed, the hakas came from every ridge.'[4] Yet another Māori soldier was hit while he was asleep, fortunately with his mouth open; he bullet entered his open mouth and lodged in his cheek with the tip poking out.[5]

The Māori soldiers also earned the respect of their commanding officers. General Sir Ian Hamilton remarked that General Godley's divisions, 'faced death with joyous alacrity as if it was some form of exciting recreation …'[6] Lieutenant Colonel Hughes noted, 'I was very pleased indeed to have the Maoris in my battalion, as they are always cheerful, keen to be taught, wonderfully alert in the trenches, willing workers when on fatigue … in fact they are an object lesson to us white Maoris.'[7]

Wiremu had hoped to return home and visit friends and family before he sailed for the war. However, by late August he was still waiting for leave to be granted and hoped that he might get home in September. Perhaps if he had been free to return home for leave before sailing for Egypt, he might have learned of Phoebe's pregnancy. However, circumstances prevented the home visit and he was destined to sail without learning of her condition.

> Maori Camp
> August 21st 1915
> Miss Virgie Fincham.
>
> Dear Virgie,
> Your most welcome letters to hand and I was pleased to hear from you. I received papers today and I noticed that several Ellesmere boys are leaving for Trentham for training for the Front. I am leaving on extended leave in a fortnight.

Next week we are leaving for target practice at Penrose, a distance of ten miles across Auckland. I might mention that target practice is our final elementary drill prior to leaving NZ. As a 2nd reinforcement Comp. has already been chosen, we are leaving very soon.

Last night the boys from the B Company gave a concert. And it was a huge success. Jimmy Pohio sang Colleen Bawn, what I liked best was the Maori Haka. Old Phillip's[8] hakas wouldn't hold a candle to the boys up here. They are simply lovely. There was a big party from Devonport and a combined concert will be held very shortly in aid of the Wounded Soldiers' Fund to be held in Devonport.

I received a letter from Daddy Pohio last week, written from Malta, dated June 13th, he says that they were expecting to be sent to the front at any time, as you are aware they have commenced operations against the Turks.

Dear Virgie. If you will care to have a photo of the South Island group like the two I sent Hinewai, let me know at once. The boys have great fun up here, when general leave is granted they go to Auckland from 2 p.m. until 10.30 p.m. on Fridays. They get pretty full; several boys have been sent home disgraced through drunkenness. Last Sunday afternoon I went to Onehunga for a look around. I and a friend of mine are going out to visit the Auckland Zoo, which is supposed to be very interesting and pretty. Well, as I have to hurry and prepare for night drill I will have to close my short letter with kind remembrance and Arohanui.

Yours sincerely
Bill

The 1st Contingent of 500 Māori men insisted on fighting alongside the Pākehā soldiers. They suffered heavy losses at the battle of Gallipoli. In late August the surviving men of the 1st Māori Contingent were divided and distributed among the other battalions.

In September the orders came through for the 2nd Māori Contingent to set sail for Egypt. Some 300 soldiers attended a civic farewell in front of the Auckland Town Hall before travelling to Wellington. Another civic farewell was held for them at the Wellington Town Hall.

The 2nd Contingent sailed from Wellington on the troopship *Waitemata* on 19 September 1915. Wiremu's sister Hinewai travelled to Wellington to farewell her brother. He was on his way to war.

Farewelling the 2nd Māori Contingent outside the Auckland Town Hall.
Auckland Libraries, Sir George Grey Special Collections, AWNS-19150923-64-2

The 2nd Māori Contingent is farewelled in Wellington.
Auckland Libraries, Sir George Grey Special Collections, AWNS-19150923-35-2

The Last Maopo

Troopship Waitemata
7/10/15

Dear Virgie,

Just a few lines to let you know that I am still alive and well and I have been very fortunate so far not being sea sick, although I was a little giddy one day. A day's rest from parade I soon recovered and now I'm a full blown sailor. I daresay you have already read in the papers the time we had in Wellington before we left there, and I was very pleased to see Hinewai there to bid me farewell. Really it was heartbreaking to me when I saw her on the Wharf when we were leaving. However I soon got over it. I am now as happy as Larry with nothing but the wide ocean around to gaze upon. A few porpoises diving up and down occasionally, as we sail along, help to keep one from pining for home and friends.

Well, as all our letters have to be passed by the Censor and not being allowed to write concerning our strength, condition and our destination, I have no news to tell you, but oh, how I wish I was at home for the Shows. I hope you will have a good time. I have met a fellow on board who worked for Patrick at Outram, and we had a great talk about show horses, he remembers seeing some of your best show horses down south, he also remembers Sandy Salter.

How are all the boys getting along? Tell old Tom that he's not to forget to send me a piece of his cake when he gets married, and I hope to be able to return and congratulate him. I suppose he has started to train his trotters now, and Johnny is pretty busy with the cows. Well Virgie, if you can send me an old Weekly Press occasionally I would be very much obliged to you, as news from New Zealand would be very acceptable.

As I have no more news to say for the present, I will now close with remembrance to all at Willow Glen and Arohanui,
From yours sincerely, friend Bill

PS please find enclosed my full address, and when addressing please put On Active Service on envelope.

Meanwhile, the Māori soldiers of the 1st Contingent had left Gallipoli on 4 October for a rest break at Mudros. Their Pākehā comrades carried their packs to the boat to see them off, and shook their hands in an emotion-filled, silent gesture where no words could adequately convey the aroha felt for the experiences they had shared.[9]

On 26 October, the *Waitemata* arrived at Suez carrying the 2nd Contingent. The soldiers went into camp 140 km inland at Zeitoun, Cairo.[10] The arrival of the new troops was warmly welcomed by the Māori survivors of the 1st Contingent.

Wiremu had a chance to catch up on news of his friends from Taumutu who had been fighting with the 1st Contingent.

Egypt
19/12/15

Dear Virgie
I received your letter of the 7th Nov. today and was very pleased to hear from you. Thanks very much for the Xmas Card and the hearty greetings you sent me. Really I enjoyed my trip very much and the sea made no affect on me whatever. At present, I am enjoying the very best of health.
Yesterday, 18th, I had a great surprise in meeting Joe Teihoka in the New Zealand general Hospital at Pont de Koubeh near Cairo. He was overtaken with dysentery and had to leave the firing line he told me. He has been two weeks today in the Hospital and is looking very sick and thin of course. He was never very stout before he enlisted, but at present he is nothing but a mere skeleton. He told me that Daddy was still on the Peninsula when he left. You can imagine my feelings when I met Joe after I heard all sorts of yarns that he was dead and again I heard that he was sent back to New Zealand on sick leave. However Virg, he and I soon settled down to a good old chat of old times and of the dear people we love so well in dear old Taumutu, of whom we are proud to fight for. Poor Joe was never informed about the death of his Mother and I had to tell him, which was rather a difficult matter.

Well Virgie, as all letters are being censored before posted I am unable to say much concerning our Camp life, strength and movements and how long we are here for. I have met several Leeston and Ellesmere district boys. Tell the boss that I have met Ralph Coe and he is looking very thin, not long out of the Hospital suffering from pneumonia and doing light duties at present. I hope you got my parcel I sent you. It is very cold here at night now that the winter is approaching. Tell the boss I was very pleased to see his name conspicuously amongst the prize-winners at the Leeston Show. A list was sent over from Leeston to Tommy Redmond of Doyleston. How are all the boys? Remember me to them all. Tell old Tom Patterson that I am expecting to see him here and that it's his duty to enlist. I don't suppose he will come though.

A fortnight ago I went to see a football match in Cairo in aid of the Red-Cross fund played between a team of NZ Artillerymen and our boys. It resulted in a win for our boys, 14 to 10 points, and it was a hard fought match. Friday Dec 17th last our boys played the New Zealand 7th Reinforcements. Our boys were defeated by 5 to 3 points.

There are some very beautiful sights to be seen near Cairo. I'm not in love with Cairo by any means, it's too dirty. Well Virgie, I am going to see Joe this afternoon and wishing you all a very Happy New Year and hoping this will find you all well. Kind remembrance to Granny, the Boss and all the boys. Hoping you will have a very prosperous harvest: the bugles have just been sounded for dinner. I will now close with best wishes and Arohanui. Kia Ora

Yours sincerely Friend Bill

Wiremu's letter was well received in Taumutu, and extracts were printed in the *Ellesmere Guardian*, particularly on account of Wiremu's reports of having seen Private Joe Teihoka who had recently been reported to have died.

One of the Māori contingents on parade.
Auckland War Memorial Museum Tamaki Paenga Hira, Album 382, p. 22

5

Phoebe goes to the Bethany Home

On the other side of the world, Phoebe was facing a battle of her own. Phoebe's parents had made arrangements for her to go to the Salvation Army Bethany Home for unwed mothers in Wellington, before her pregnancy began to show. There were few options available to her and she went along with the plan to stay at the maternity home in the latter stage of her pregnancy.

Before she left for the maternity home, Phoebe's parents told her they had received news that Wiremu had been killed in the war. This fabrication was a means of discouraging any relationship between the two. Phoebe's parents planned to register the birth in their own names and adopt the child out so Phoebe could go on to marry with a clean record. Phoebe, however, had no intention of giving up her child.

Phoebe arrived at Bethany Home on 6 December 1915, almost six months into her pregnancy. She discovered there were two categories for pregnant mothers. The unmarried pregnant mothers, or 'inmates' as they were described, were made to clean, scrub floors, sew, wash sheets and work in the maternity home. According to Phoebe, they were not permitted to eat the same meals as married mothers; they instead had bread and golden syrup for tea.

Conditions for the 'inmates' were worse than for the married mothers. Phoebe later said that they were not allowed any form of anaesthetic during labour, as punishment for their sins. Unafraid of hard work, Phoebe settled in. Her independent and adventurous nature stood her in good stead to deal with the difficult circumstances at the home.

While Phoebe was adjusting to her new surroundings and working through her pregnancy, Wiremu continued to keep the families at Taumutu informed of his activities in Egypt, unaware of her situation. The *Ellesmere Guardian* published an extract of another one of his letters so the local community could keep track of his progress:

8 January 1916

A Maori Soldier's Letter — Preparing To Do His Little Bit
Among the young men who joined the reinforcements for the Maori Contingent was a member of a well-known Taumutu family, Private William K. Maopo. By a recent mail, a scholar of the Sedgemere School received a letter from Private Maopo, from Zeitoun Camp, Egypt, in the course of which the writer says:

'Having a little spare time at my disposal, I now take the opportunity of dropping you a line to let you know that I am doing well. We are getting a lot of hard work — out drilling on the desert from 6 to 8.30 in the morning, rout marching from breakfast till dinner time, then rifle shooting. We are leaving shortly for an island in the Mediterranean Sea called Lemnos, where many of our New Zealand boys of the first contingent are having a spell until we are sent to reinforce them. I have been told that Henry Pohio is there. Joe Teihoka, I hear, has died of sickness, but I am not able to say whether this is correct or not. I am always on the look-out for boys from Canterbury. Allan Lamont is the only chap from the Ellesmere district I have met so far and I had a great chat with him.

Cairo is about eight miles from our camp and we are often there sight-seeing. There are some great buildings in Cairo but I am not greatly struck with the town. The chief inhabitants are Arabs, Egyptians and blacks. The native quarter is very filthy and the *natives try to sell fruit that one wouldn't have the heart to give to the pigs in New Zealand. They don't forget to ask big prices for everything.*

Last Sunday I visited the Soldiers' Home in Cairo, which is a very big building. All sorts of nice drinks and fruit can be had there and there are plenty of games to indulge in. There are also plenty of New Zealand papers to read. By the time you get this letter I shall be at the front doing my bit. I would like to be home for Christmas, but better luck next time, perhaps.

I am looking forward to a lot of mail from home. Have to go out on piquet tonight so good-bye.'

Private Maopo was employed for a number of years by Mr H.E. Fincham of Willow Glen and, in a postscript to his letter, he makes inquiries concerning Mr Fincham's stud Clydesdales and their successes in the show rings.

On 18 January the 2nd Māori Contingent arrived from Zeitoun to join the depleted ranks of the 1st Contingent. The 1st Contingent welcomed the new soldiers in true Māori fashion under the leadership of Captain Buck, and the 2nd Contingent responded in kind under the leadership of Lieutenant Kohere. After the pōwhiri, the soldiers caught up with old mates and news from home, with the new recruits looking clean and tidy in their new clothes, alongside the well-worn uniforms of the 1st Contingent.[1]

The Māori soldiers of the 1st Contingent who survived the eight-month battle of Gallipoli were divided up and allocated as platoons (groups of 26 to 64) across the infantry battalions (groups of 300 to 1300). The 2nd Contingent was similarly divided when they arrived, and the soldiers were allocated across the infantry battalions. The Māori soldiers protested against the integration with the rest of the New Zealand Division and pressed for a separate Māori Battalion.

Wiremu was stationed in Egypt for five months before activities for relocation began. Amid the training and preparations there were occasional opportunities for recreation and entertainment.

The Canal
Jan 28th 1916

Dear Virgie

Just a few lines of Arohanui to inform you that I received your most kind & welcome letter of Dec 14th 1915 yesterday 27th. I was very pleased to hear from an old friend & you can hardly imagine how it makes one feel cheerful when he receives a letter from old acquaintances. Thanks awfully for the Weekly Press you sent me. I also received busters from Len a few days after your paper arrived.

The 2nd Maori Contingent has been drafted with the 1st Maoris into the Pakeha Infantry Battalions of NZ. All the South Island boys and those boys from the North Island who are with us South Islanders are attached to the Wellington Infantry Battalion, that is to say one Platoon of Maoris is attached to each individual Battalion. Last Sunday 23rd the whole Maori Contingent paraded for Church conducted by our own Chaplains. Generals Godley & Russell with Staff Officers were in attendance after church. General Godley, who is in command of all New Zealand Infantry Brigades in Egypt, inspected our Contingent. He also spoke words of great appreciation for the good work our 1st Maoris have already done & the deeds they performed when on the Peninsula and hoped that the Maori Reinforcements would also acquit themselves when called upon alongside their Pakeha brothers, which I think we will do.

Dear Virgie, I am pleased to hear that Bertie McGill is coming over to join the boys. Only fancy he is the only brave boy from Sedgemere coming. I met Billy Simpson and Jim Jones and Capt. Hammond, an old Leeston boy, he is second in command of the South Canterbury Mounted Brigade. In fact, I met several old boys from the Ellesmere district, too numerous to mention. I have not visited Joe Teihoka since I wrote last nor heard anything concerning him. H. Pohio is at present holding the rank of Sergeant Major for our Company of 2 Platoons. I am more than pleased to see in the busters of what the lady-folks are *doing to help the boys at the front. Please tell Tom I am looking forward to meeting him out here. All letters are strictly censored here and I am unable to write more that what's necessary. I am enjoying the best of health & hoping you are all the same.*

Kind remembrance to all at Willow Glen and hoping to hear from you again at your earliest and may God's blessing be bestowed upon you all until we meet again.

Yours sincerely

Friend   Pte W.K. Maopo

Egypt

Henry Pohio.
Newspaper clipping supplied by Joan Overhill.

Wiremu was posted to a unit at Moascar, Ismailia, Egypt, on 20 January 1916. The survivors of the 1st Māori Contingent had continued to request that they be united with the 2nd Māori Contingent reinforcements to reinstate Te Hokowhitu a Tū. Their requests were given due consideration and, on 20 February 1916, orders were issued to form a New Zealand Pioneer Battalion from men of the 1st and 2nd Māori contingents, along with men from the Otago Mounted Rifles, as there were not enough Māori soldiers to form a full Battalion. The Māori Pioneers were organised into A, B, C and D companies based on tribal groupings, and Pākehā soldiers from the Otago Mounted Rifles were allocated to each of the four companies. It was hoped that over time there would be enough soldiers to form a full Māori battalion.

Wiremu was assigned to C Company, which comprised Māori soldiers from Te Arawa, Bay of Plenty, East Coast, Taupo and the South Island. The C Company Māori officers were Lieutenant Stainton and 2nd Lieutenant Walker of the 1st Contingent, and 2nd lieutenants Kohere and Masters of the 2nd Contingent.[2]

While stationed at Moascar, Wiremu continued to write to Virgie with regular updates of their activities.

> *Moascar Camp*
> *Feb 29th 1916*
>
> *Dear Virgie*
> *I have again taken the opportunity of replying to your ever kind and welcome letter of Jan. 2nd, which again found me enjoying the best of health. I was extremely pleased to hear that you are all keeping well. Trusting such will be the case until we all meet again. I am also pleased to receive the paper you sent me. It fairly cheered me, and I may say that a letter or any paper from some dear old friends in good old NZ always helps one a great lot to while away the evenings. Also to know that there are some far away from this wearisome, sandy land called Egypt. I have not a great lot of news to relate, but as I am writing these few lines in the YMCA writing room, the 'Australian Field Ambulance Corps' are giving a lovely concert, in return to one given by the Maori Contingent Concert Party*

several weeks ago, as a farewell parting, to the 'Australians' who were attached to the NZ Division, now being transferred back to their own Division, camped some distance away from us.

I may say the New Zealand boys were always on good terms with the Australians while attached to us. There is also a football tournament being played over here, several good teams representing the different units from New Zealand now serving in Egypt at the present time, including several representative players from New Zealand who have won Caps on the field in their respective provinces and New Zealand generally.

Our regiment is represented by a very strong team. Wellington leading, our team has only lost one game so far. I will let you know the result later on when the tournament has finished. At present the boys are having really good times drilling only in the forenoons, we put the rest of the day in washing our clothes or mending. Cigarettes and tobacco are pretty plentiful. The Over-Seas Club send boxes in galore for the boys.

I read from a cutting in the paper I had sent to me regarding the great presentation and send off to Bertie McGill given in the old shed. I can fully realise the good time spent. Ah, what a good time we boys missed, however I think a better time is coming later on, when this war is over and the conquering heroes go back to old New Zealand once more.

Well Virgie, I daresay this will be getting rather uninteresting and as this is my eighth letter since tea I must ask you to excuse the short letter and scarcity of news, more to follow later on. Sergt. Major H. Pohio is well and wished to be remembered to all. I enclose with remembrance and arohanui to all at Willow Glen.

Yours sincerely
Pte W.K. Maopo
O.A.S.O
Egypt

PS Tell Granny I still think of her sometimes and wonder how she's keeping. Bill.

On 6 March the Māori Pioneers marched to camp south of the Moascar aerodrome. Their early days at the camp were spent on exercises, fatigues, parades and rugby practice. On 12 March the Māori team challenged the Wellington Battalion for the Rugby championship and lost 3–0.

On 15 March the Pioneers received orders to move east of the Canal, alongside the Reserve Camp. The following day the 3rd Māori Contingent arrived at Suez and travelled to Ismalia by train, where they were met by Lieutenant Dansey and marched to the Reserve Camp. The men had contracted measles on the voyage so they were immediately put into isolation. After six days of quarantine they were cleared to join their colleagues and were allocated to Companies.[3]

The Pioneers' days were occupied with desert drills, route marching and training. The desert conditions provided new challenges for the men. When the strong desert winds came up the air filled with sand and blew the tents down. Sections of the men marched out with camel transports to clear the sand from the trenches.

On 21 March orders were received to break camp and march back to Moascar. Once the camp was packed and the wagons were loaded, the Battalion was inspected by His Royal Highness The Prince of Wales. Lieutenant Kohere led Ngāti Porou soldiers in a haka in the Prince's honour.

First World War photograph of Māori soldiers performing a haka in Egypt. JM, fl 1915, photograph taken by J.M. Price, William Archer, 1866–1948: Collection of postcard negatives. Alexander Turnbull Library, Wellington, New Zealand, Ref. 1/2-000580-G

6

Phoebe's baby

Phoebe gave birth to a baby girl at Bethany Home on 8 March 1916. She named her daughter Marjorie Joyce. In naming her daughter, she followed a pattern of using matching initials in her family lineage: her mother's name was Harriet Hill (HH); her name was Phoebe Prentice (PP); and her daughter was Marjorie, which if given her father's surname, Maopo, meant her initials were MM.

Sadly, baby Marjorie Joyce entered the world just as her grandfather, Atarea Te Maiharanui Maopo, left the world at age 80. He died two weeks after her birth. In Māori tradition the coincidence of a tupuna dying and a mokopuna being born at the same time generally indicates a special bond or connection between the two, a spiritual transference from one to the other. How pleased Atarea would have been if he had known that with his passing a new generation of the Maopo family was beginning.

Phoebe and her baby were without family at the maternity home in Wellington. Phoebe was delighted with her baby daughter and was determined not to be parted from her. She knew that they were alone in the world as her parents would not let her return home with the baby, and they had told her that Wiremu had been killed in the war. She had no option but to stay on at Bethany Home.

In fact, Wiremu had celebrated his birthday in Egypt on 17 March, not knowing that he had become a father and that his own father was close to passing.

On 4 April General Murray inspected the Māori Pioneers at camp. The Pākehā platoons formed a line around the Māori Pioneers and, once again, Lieutenant Kohere led C Company in haka. The Rarotongan soldiers supported with their haka and marching songs. Major Buck gave a welcome address and General Murray responded, expressing his satisfaction of the Battalion and its work.[1]

On 5 April orders were received to leave Egypt, and the troops set about preparing for the move to the battle zone. They sailed on the transport ship *Canada* from Egypt to Marseilles, and then travelled in a packed train for two to three days. The French countryside provided them with a welcome change of scenery from the hot, dry deserts of Egypt. The troops disembarked at St Omer and marched to Morbeque and on to Sercus.

On 30 April a tree-chopping competition was held between Māori and French bushmen. Each team had to fell 12 trees in the French style of cutting the tree off level with the ground and trimming the stump to leave a rounded top. The Māori bushmen beat the French team by three minutes, despite the unusual cutting technique. The next day the Battalion marched 17 miles with full packs to Estaires.[2]

The following days were spent performing short route marches, bayonet fighting, gas alarm practices and physical drills. The troops also found time for rugby practice, and the Pioneer XV played the Welsh at Lavantie, beating them 18 to 4.

On 15 May the Pioneer Battalion received orders to move to Armentières, a combat zone. After a period of further training in construction and maintenance of wire entanglements, dugouts, shelters and trenches, Wiremu's company was assigned to work on support and subsidiary lines, and communications for front line trenches. Work was done at night only as it was considered unsafe to move the parties into the trenches during daylight. When the companies arrived back at camp they would record any casualties. All trenches were in a very bad state and it looked like they had months of work ahead.

On 21 May the commanding officer went to see the wood-chopping competition at Forêt de Nieppe between teams from the Canadian, Australian and New Zealand divisions. The Māori team represented New Zealand in taking on some of the best wood choppers in the world. From the four competitions they won two and came second in the other two.³

Letters during this period were infrequent and it was two or three months before Wiremu had the opportunity to write to Virgie again:

> Somewhere in France
> May 20th 1916
>
> Dear Virgie
> Kindly accept this as a token of old friendship and for the days of Auld Lang Syne. Bill.
> Ladies small fancy hooked handkerchief.

> Somewhere in France
> 23/5/16
>
> Dear Virgie
> I am more than pleased to receive the paper today. Thanks awfully as we have been wandering about a lot. I had not much time to write today, however being an off day for the army I managed to find time to thank you for the paper and also to say that I am enjoying the very best of health at present, although when we first arrived we felt the cold very keenly but we are quite used to the weather conditions, which is very much like NZ weather. Tell the boys I have not had the pleasure of meeting Harrington yet. I made enquiries but have not managed to meet him.
> I have not much to say just now but we are pretty well treated. Leave on Furlough to England has been granted and several of our boys have been over and others are over there at present.
> How is everybody keeping on the old farm? Kind remembrance to Granny and all the boys. Fall in has just been sounded so I will have to enclose with arohanui.
>
> Yours sincerely
> Pte W.K. Maopo

On pay days the Māori soldiers liked to partake of a few beers accompanied by a singalong on the piano. Major King tried to discourage the men from what he considered to be 'disorderly conduct' by regularly dishing out 28-day stays in the army jail. Wiremu took part in the occasional celebration.

> Somewhere in France
> May 27th 1916
>
> Dear Virgie
> Your letter of March 6th and parcel to hand today. I thank you very much for sending same which I greatly appreciated. I have also to thank you for your kind birthday greetings. Now I must tell you how I celebrated that event. We were still in Egypt when the 17th came round. I happened to meet another fellow the evening before, in the soldiers' canteen, and while speaking on different matters of the evening he mentioned that the next day was his birthday, St Pat's day. I told him my birthday was also on the next day, how we laughed and planned to have a real good time.
> That evening, sure enough, we both met at 7 p.m. I had five shillings and he had a pound. So I asked him what to do to begin with. He suggested I was to buy the beer and he'll stand for biscuits, tinned beef and milk. I bought a bucket full of beer and we both drank each other's health and hoped to celebrate our next birthdays in old New Zealand next year. However, I can only say that we had a really good night but next morning I had rather a swelled head and, as we were leaving camp that day for the trenches near the canal, I felt rather out of sorts. However, I managed to march away with the rest of the boys. So much for St Pat's day.
>
> Dear Virgie I hope this will find you all well at home, as it leaves me the same at present. Things are awfully quiet over here just now. I have not met any of the district boys for a long time. We are all scattered about over here and it is very hard to find any of

the boys until you run right across them. Cannon is the only one I have met two or three times since we landed in France. He is now in the trenches. I heard the other day that Ernie Williams from Leeston received a shrapnel wound and is now in the first aid hospital.

I suppose you have seen in the papers where one of our officers got shot recently and three other men were slightly wounded while in the trenches. We were sorry to lose him but however, I suppose it cannot be helped.

Has Joe arrived down there yet? And Huri I believe has also been sent back to New Zealand for feet troubles. Hoping to hear that you are all keeping well at your earliest. Arohanui to all at home.

Yours sincerely
Bill.

Some weeks after landing in France, Wiremu received the sad news that his father had died on 22 March 1916, aged 80. He had passed away merely six months after Wiremu had sailed from New Zealand and a few days after Wiremu had celebrated his 30th birthday.

In the combat zone conditions were considerably more serious, and the cold winter weather added a further element of hardship. Finding it too difficult to adapt to the climate, 150 Niuean soldiers were sent home. During May the Battalion started to take on casualties and sadly, two officers were killed.[4]

Somewhere in France
30th May 1916

Dear Virgie
It has again given me great pleasure to reply to your letter of April 9th which I received today.
I forgot to tell you in my last letter that the chocolates were excellent and arrived in good condition. I had it all to myself as Daddy was away to the Bomb School. I couldn't wait for him. They were just alright, I can assure you.

Well Virgie I am sorry to hear of the death of John Lochhead I assure you. George and Jessie will find it very lonely without their father. Please convey to them my heartfelt condolence in their sad bereavement.

I have also received today a letter from Hinewai announcing the death of Father, who died at Little River on March 22nd. Well, I got a terrible shock. Although he was well on in years, I never dreamt of him going off sickly and so today all my sympathies are with them, whose loved ones have been taken away and I am sure that Hinewai will very much miss me now that Father is dead. So I sincerely hope that I may have the good fortune to be able to return home after the war.

Virgie, things are pretty lively over here at present. Where we are based the Germans can send over shells without any difficulty, and several soldiers have received wounds while walking about in the town of an evening before heading for the trenches, which we do just at dusk, and the Germans usually send over shells between 5.30 and 6 o'clock, just about the time the boys are out. I can only say that one is very lucky indeed if ever he escapes with a wound, for the Germans are pretty good shots. Our Battalion has already lost the services of two officers, one shot outright, the other died of wounds, and there are four men slightly wounded. I have been twice in the trenches and I'm not in love with it either. One has to keep his head well down off the parapet otherwise he'll be spotted.

I am now acting as messenger on the Battalion headquarters staff. I like it very much. You have much more liberty running about the town delivering messages and there are no fatigues or other work to do. You are also provided bicycles to ride, only the roads are very bad, that is to say all the roads are paved with bricks and are nothing but hills and hollows, which make it very unpleasant. Well Virgie, I suppose by the time you receive this letter I'll have returned from England on Furlough and I'll be able to write and tell you all about the place when I write again. From all accounts, I hear those who have already visited England and Scotland speak very highly of the countries and the people for entertaining them.

> Well, I have already told you all the news I can think of just now. I will now close with kind remembrance and arohanui to all at home. Please remember me to Emily when writing again.
>
> I am yours sincerely friend Bill.

Wiremu had continued to write to Phoebe but no reply to his letters ever came. He regrettably accepted that she had moved on and eventually he stopped writing to her. He was unaware of the struggles that had befallen Phoebe shortly after he had departed.

Phoebe's parents had wanted Phoebe to agree to an adoption for the baby so that she could continue with her life. They proposed the baby's birth to be registered to Phoebe's mother Harriet, so it would look as if Harriet had had another child, and there would be no record of Phoebe ever having had a child. This would mean her chances of making a good marriage would not be harmed.

As part of the plan to ensure that she made a new life for herself and put her 'mistakes' behind her, Phoebe's family had deceived her by telling her that Wiremu had died in the war. Phoebe was devastated. Her parents arranged for the baby's birth certificate to list Harriet as the mother and father as 'unknown'.

Despite her grief, her lack of options, and the sustained efforts of her parents, Phoebe would not agree to give up her baby. She refused to sign the consent papers. She might have lost Wiremu, but she had no intention of losing their daughter as well.

After giving birth to Marjorie Joyce, Phoebe stayed on with her baby for eight months, working at Bethany Home. She had nowhere else to go. She refused to adopt out her baby and the options were limited for a young girl in her position. Marjorie Joyce was a beautiful, healthy baby and Phoebe was devoted to her.

During her time at Bethany Home, Phoebe engaged in various household duties and sewing. The home was frequently overcrowded, especially in the nursery and dormitories. She saw many other young girls come and go and formed many special friendships.

A full year on from her arrival at Bethany Home a telegram eventually came. Within was the news for which Phoebe had hoped.

Her parents conceded she could return home and bring the baby. The telegram from her father read: 'COME HOME WITH BABY'. Finally, Phoebe could leave the maternity home without having to give up her baby. On 15 November 1916, with relief and excitement, Phoebe boarded the train for Palmerston North with her baby daughter Marjorie Joyce. She said farewell to staff at Bethany Home and looked forward to the next stage of her life.

Phoebe saw her parents standing on the train station platform and disembarked from the train to proudly introduce the new grandparents to their new granddaughter. She handed the baby into their arms knowing their hearts would soften at the first sight of this precious baby girl.

However, with little regard for the baby, Phoebe's parents introduced a third person on the platform who they said would be the baby's nanny. Shock descended over Phoebe as she watched her parents hand the baby over to the waiting arms of this stranger, and then felt them hold her back while the stranger fled from the platform with the baby. Phoebe was distraught. Her struggles, screams and cries were useless as she failed to break free from the firm grip of her parents. Her baby was abducted into the night.

While Phoebe was fighting for their daughter in Palmerston North, Wiremu was fighting for his country in France. Circumstances had separated them from each other, and from their child, and separated the new baby from her parents.

After being whisked away from the train station, Marjorie Joyce was delivered into the arms of a waiting man with whom an adoption had been arranged. Marjorie was adopted by Edward Clemans and Elizabeth May Harman, who were living in Hamilton. They were kind people and already had a daughter, Vera, aged 6, and a son, Clemens, aged 8. They called Marjorie by her middle name, Joyce. Vera and Clemens were surprised when their father came home one night with a new baby. Nothing was said about where the baby had come from. She became their new sister.

The Harman family later had another daughter, Eunice. They were a good family and they took good care of Marjorie Joyce.

♥ The Last *Maopo*

```
        Edward Clemans Harman  =  Elizabeth May Harman
        ┌──────────────┬───────────────┬──────────────┐
       Thomas        Marjorie        Marjorie        Eunice
       Edward        Vera Jane        Joyce          Violet
       Clemens                       (adopted)


                     Phoebe  =  Bill England
                              │
                             Betty
```

Whakapapa Chart 5

7

A world at war

The worlds between Phoebe, Wiremu and Marjorie Joyce continued to grow further and further apart.

While Phoebe was struggling with the loss of her daughter, the Taumutu ladies were busy preparing parcels to send the men at the Front. The Sedgemere Social Committee packed parcels to be dispatched to Wiremu Maopo, Henry Pohio, George Taiaroa, Fred Stretz and Reg Thian. Each parcel contained a plum pudding, fruit cake, coffee and milk, chocolates, cigarettes and a writing set. Granny also provided a parcel of socks to be included in the package.

The engagement with the fighting at the Western Front had kept Wiremu busy with little time to write home, and it was some months before friends and family heard from him again. In June 1916, the Pioneers were engaged in routine work laying telephone wires, digging trenches and milling timber. Each company was allocated a portion of the defensive line to protect and hold in the event of attack. The work was increasingly dangerous. Lieutenant Walker, Wiremu's Commanding Officer, was sent to hospital after losing two fingers at the sawmill; Sergeant Delamere was accidentally killed at the bomb school where he was acting as an instructor, and many soldiers were wounded or killed after being severely shelled while working.[1]

The Pioneers were involved in night raids on the German trenches. Their mission was to capture machine guns and trench mortars, secure two prisoners for identification, and kill as many Germans as possible.

The Last *Maopo*

The soldiers were instructed to wear light clothes with no New Zealand buttons or identification, and to carry bombs and Māori meres but no rifles. They were to blacken their faces and undertake to speak only in Māori. Volunteers for the Māori night raids were far in excess of the numbers required.[2]

In August 1916, Wiremu's company continued working on dugouts, drainage and trenches in Armentières, with a selection of men from each company training to become bomb throwers. Shelling was a regular event, so the men worked in the early hours of the morning, moving about freely under the cover of the morning mist.

One of Wiremu's letters published in the *Ellesmere Guardian* talked about a visit to the troops by Sir James Carroll:

21/10/16

Maori Soldier's letter - Sir James Carroll's visit to France
Private W.K. Maopo, a well-known Taumutu boy, has written an interesting letter to a resident of Sedgemere, from which the following extracts were taken.

'We are having excellent weather here just now (Aug. 9th), and the big guns are roaring very frequently. Quite recently we had the Hon. Sir James Carroll over here to see us, and we had a day's holiday given us for the occasion. We all turned out spic and span, with everything clean and neat, boots shining and buttons glittering. Our haka party greeted Sir James with a cry, and then Major Buck made a speech of welcome. We were very pleased to see Sir James, for his presence reminded us of those we long to see once again at home. When he stood up to speak he made touching reference to those who had fallen on the heights of Gallipoli and here in France and urged us to be determined to see this war through.
Last Sunday evening a concert was held in our billet to commemorate the anniversary of the first charge of the Māori Contingent made on Gallipoli, and it proved quite a success. A few French civilians were present, including some very pretty

> Mademoiselles. They remained until some of the boys gave the famous war cry and they then appeared to be fairly frightened out of their wits and left soon after it was finished. Some nice patriotic songs were sung and we had quite a good evening's entertainment.
>
> I expected some time ago to get away on a visit to England, but a change was made and all leave was cancelled indefinitely as all available men were wanted. I was very much disappointed as my turn was very close. Rumour has it that leave will be granted again very shortly. We are at a great disadvantage in not knowing the French language. If we could only speak it, we would get along splendidly. Out of our whole battalion there are not six who could speak French fluently. I know only a few words of French — it's worse than Māori . There is one boy here with us who can speak six different languages and he gets on well with the French people. We have just received our new regimental badges — that is our pioneer battalion badge. It is a very good design. Last week I met Ted Anderson (Leeston) out in the trenches. He only recently came out of hospital but is as cheery as ever.

Orders were received to move further south. But because orders were badly arranged, the Pioneers' wagons arrived late at the starting point and the officers reported that the march out looked more like a circus than a regiment first-line transport on the move.

The units moved from Armentières to Étaples. The long marches were hard on the men as they had come from three months of trench work. Their boots were in bad shape and their feet suffered. Much of the footwear had been remade from secondhand boots and caused foot problems. From Étaples the men travelled to the Somme, continuing their trench and dugout work in wet conditions and amidst attacks and shelling.

These were grim conditions. On 12 September, the War Diary entry recorded the following:

> The country between Black Watch Trench and the German front line is in an awful state. The shell craters are so thick that they

> overlap one another and there are dead of both sides lying unburied all over the place — some have been dead since the cavalry first took Highwood in July.
>
> The trenches are nothing but a wreck and no one seems to consider it his job to clean them up. Truly the British are a wonderful people. They would rather sit in a busted trench and get shot than do a little work on the end of a pick and shovel.

The soldiers often went out at daylight to find their previous day's work destroyed and the areas strewn with fallen men. The Pioneers suffered many casualties during this period.

Wiremu wrote regularly to his sister, Hinewai, and Virgie Fincham, and he sent the odd letter to the Leeston community newspaper. Wiremu's letters now reflected a more serious state of affairs as the soldiers were fully engaged at the Western Front and had just come off the Battle of the Somme, where the Pioneer Battalion suffered heavy losses, but had earned a reputation as fighting soldiers. Major King reported losing over 200 men from the Pioneer Battalion. Wiremu was lucky to avoid misfortune during this time.

> France
> 9/11/16
>
> Dear Virgie
> No doubt you will be wondering what's become of me, whether I'm still alive. Well, truth to say that I'm very much alive but owing to the fact that our boys were too busy on the Western Front helping to win back what was taken last year and also travelling from place to place, I hadn't much time to write any earlier to reply to your letter of July which I received quite recently.
>
> Well I have not much news to write about, only that I'm very pleased to be able to say that I was one of the lucky ones to leave the Western Front untouched, though we had many casualties. I am now with our transport, driving mules or rather riding them as leaders in front of one wagon attached to the Company I belong to.

How are all the folks keeping around Sedgemere and Taumutu? All well I hope. I have not had the pleasure of meeting your cousin out here, as we are all scattered about, it's very difficult to find them. I have not even met Bertie McGill since I've been here in France. As a matter of fact I've lost the whole run of all my old comrades from Southbridge and round Leeston districts. What sort of a show did you people have at Leeston this year? I hope the Boss did the hat trick with some of the young Auchencruives.

The winter is fast approaching over here now and we have been getting plenty of wet weather and the mud is awful. I believe the winter over here is very cold and is supposed to last quite six months, so I'm picking myself to catch a lovely dose of influenza, which would just about finish me for the duration of the war.

Well Virgie, I think I will now conclude with Arohanui and a hearty greeting for a Merry Xmas and Happy New Year to you all. Kind remembrance to all on the old farm.

I remain yours sincerely

Pte. W.K. Maopo
Address 16/658
Pte. W.K. Maopo
No.3 Platoon
'A' Coy
NZld Pioneers

The work of 'A' Company during November continued. They created dugouts, drains, wiring support lines and roads, as well as building a cinema called the Ka Pai Theatre. By this time the weather had turned damp and cold, with misty days clearing in the evenings and a slight frost during the nights.

The Last *Maopo*

France
27/11/16

Dear Virgie

Today has been very cold and word has just been sent along that a big New Zealand mail has just arrived for our Battalion (Pioneers) of course. I, being one of the lucky ones, received five letters, yours of Oct 1st being one of them.

Oh you don't know how your letters, also letters from home, gladden my heart out here in this land of the Frenchman. News galore, local and general. I guess you are having some very pleasant evening socials since I came away. Just what it should be too, what say you.

How are you off for dance partners? I hear and see in the papers that several boys have come away recently. Why, if the war lasts much longer there won't be any boys left at all. I admire Taumutu and Sedgemere's energy in pushing ahead with a new Hall. My word, won't you people have dances now. How is Lakeside taking it? They were to build one years ago. Awfully pleased that the little district I am representing out here has taken the lead and hope to be spared to return and dance in your new hall, or rather ours I should say, for I believe I am a member.

Well Virgie, I have not much news to write to you this time, but the winter is going to be severe. Quite recently in getting up one morning, the ground was quite white with snow and only fancy this is only the beginning. The frost is very severe also. Rain, why it simply pours down over here so imagine how the boys are getting along in the trenches, but we are well supplied with good warm clothing. Hot bath weekly, which we enjoy immensely. A special building has been erected for this purpose. On arrival at the baths all dirty clothes are exchanged for clean after we have had our bath, so we are well looked after. Pay day fortnightly.

I have not been on the booze since I have been here but Christmas is not far off, with ordinary luck, I will probably have a tangi [hāngi]. Providing the pay book is holding, a sum is issued regularly to us all, but it's too fiery and goes to one's head too quickly.

Well Virg, pleased to hear that all is well at home and things are about the same as I left it, but only wait till the boys of the old brigade return home, guess we'll paint the old Pah red. Now that Joe is at home and married, if he, Daddy and I get together again, oh won't we have some fun.

You were alluding to hurrying back from here for a real royal time you folks will be giving. They say that the war is going for five more years yet. I think I'll be grey headed by then. I have already started to get grey. I suppose it's the fright, what say you. No man's land is not very pleasant but as I have already written and told you that I have been transferred to our transport as driver. The cold footed mob we are called out here now.

Well Virgie, Christmas only comes but once a year. Last year I sent you a table cover with our old badge embroidered from Egypt. This year I am sending a handkerchief case affair. I don't know what it's called but please accept same as a token of friendship, also as a souvenir from France. I am also sending one home to Hinewai and I hope that you would like it.

I have not been able to go away on furlough yet as my turn doesn't come for a while. Only fancy, we are told that Berlin is out of bounds to all British troops and a writer in some of the papers we have read out here thinks that give the colonial troops plenty of money guaranteed the boys will get there within three days. Of course this is merely a takeoff on account of us going out in the evenings to villages where all British troops are forbidden not to enter.

Tell Jock Patterson that I had the pleasure of meeting his brother-in-law out here only two days ago. Sam Jones. He's with the rifle brigade. He looks well. I only had a few minutes' chat with him as I was out with the wagon so I had to shorten our conversation but it does one good meeting old friends and people whom one knew in New Zealand.

Oh, Daddy and I would very much like to know who the fair haired boy is whom you alluded to when you mentioned writing to the best boy too. Trusting that we are not asking too much. However we both think that whoever he may be, he's in luck. One to be envied any time in the week.

The Last *Maopo*

I am enjoying the very best of health at present, Daddy also. We are expecting to meet George Taiaroa soon as he is over here in France. His brother Martin is with 'C. Coy' of our battalion. Having shortage of news at present I will now conclude trusting this will reach and find you all enjoying the best of health. Kind remembrance to everybody on the farm. Hoping to hear from you again soon. Arohanui until we meet again.

Yours sincerely
16/658 Driver W.K.Maopo
'A' Coy.
New Zealand Pioneers
Transport
Cl- GPO Wellington

8

Phoebe: moving on

In New Zealand, Phoebe was understandably distraught after the loss of their daughter. She received little emotional support from her parents. They had registered Marjorie Joyce as their own in order that there would be no record of Phoebe giving birth out of wedlock. In doing so they were seen as the baby's legal parents and they could authorise her adoption.

Phoebe was determined to find her child. However, first she had to find a way to create her own life and break away from her family. Devastated by her parents' cruel actions, she secured a job in a milk bar in Feilding, and took up lodgings as a boarder with a Mrs Pawson. Free of parental control, Phoebe was determined to find her baby. She relentlessly searched for clues and information that would lead her to the family that had adopted Marjorie Joyce.

Phoebe believed that Wiremu had died in the war. Although she was resolved in her determination to find their daughter, there were limited options for a young woman alone. While working in the milk bar, Phoebe met and became friends with William Wold Anderson, a Norwegian seaman who had left his home country at age 13. He had worked on ships, eventually settling in New Zealand and finding work on a farm outside of Feilding. The relationship between William and Phoebe progressed and they were married in the Feilding Baptist Church in January 1917. The reception was held in Mrs Pawson's garden. Phoebe was 19 and William was 34.

❦ The Last *Maopo*

Meanwhile, Wiremu had been in service for over a year. The war effort became more arduous with the onset of winter, but the Māori soldiers continued to find opportunities to lift their spirits.

> France
> 28/11/16
>
> Mr. H.E. Fincham Esq.
> Willow Glen
>
> Dear Herb
> Just a few hurried lines to let you know that I am still going strong out here, somewhere in France. I am enjoying the very best of health. Hoping these few lines will find you indulging the same also. Though this has been the first time I have taken the liberty of writing, I have not altogether forgotten old friends and you have been one of the best.
> Though I think when this does reach you, Christmas and New Year will have once again appeared on the scene and taken flight. I may be late in offering my heartiest greetings but better late than never, for which I now enclose card offering same. You will see in photograph or picture His Majesty the King centre left, General Russell, New Zealand right, Earl Liverpool, General Godley inspecting some of the men somewhere in France.
> We are having some very cold frosty weather here just now. No rain for some considerable time. Light fall of snow quite recently. I now conclude with remembrance to all and Kia Ora.
>
> Yours Sincerely
> Driver W.K. Maopo
> N.Zld Pioneers.

The frosts became more frequent and severe, and the Pioneers continued their work through December amid episodes of shelling. There was space for an occasional game of football and A Company sent a team to La Motte to play against the best French team. A

Company won the game 16–0. During December General Haig visited and complimented the Pioneers on their smart turnout and form marching, and also for the good work done at the Somme.

Christmas Day came and there was no work for anyone. After a church parade in the morning the Pioneers celebrated Christmas with a hāngi of pork, beef, geese and vegetables. The War Diary notes that most members of the Battalion were in a state of collapse during the afternoon.

In the following days, Wiremu wrote home to bring friends and family up to date with the past few months' experiences.

France
28/12/16

Dear Virgie
As promised I will try and write to let you know how I fared and carried on while out on the Western Front, the 'Somme'. We arrived in August and three days later our Company was sent out in the evening at 8 p.m. by motor transport to a point called the 'Crucifixion Corner', where we had to march with equipment, rifle and 120 rounds of ammunition. The roads were over our boot tops with mud and slush, the night was as dark as pitch with only flares showing us the way.
We were going out to a certain point to make a new sap or communication roadway for the infantry to move up and take their position in the front line of trenches and supports. We must have been marching for fully six hours before we were halted to take a well earned rest by the roadside. Whilst resting a Tommy, or English soldier, came along to meet us and to be our guide, he was to take us along to where we were supposed to work, however the night being dark and with a thick fog on, we were actually lost. We must have travelled twelve to sixteen miles from where we met the guide, and eventually with our officers being as much exhausted as we were they decided to retire right back to our camp. On receiving the word to retire all of us boys gave three ringing cheers which gave us heart. We returned back to

camp arriving at 5.30 a.m. the next morning absolutely tired, foot sore and hungry. After partaking of lunch and breakfast we turned in for some sleep. Oh you should have seen the state our boots, puttees and clothes were in, simply awful, enough to make one cry. Mud all over.

Having had a good rest and tea and change of clothes some of us went out to the YMCA for reading materials and supper. So ended my first experience at the Somme.

Two nights later a small party of us went out to clear a roadway of wire entanglements. This time we had not the long distances to travel but it was more dangerous owing to the fact that several big howitzers or guns were in action near us. After working for two hours we managed to complete our task which was rather an awkward job. We had not finished five minutes when Fritz commenced to shell our big gun positions so you may bet we got away from there pretty quickly, returning to camp at midnight.

Since then and prior to the time the New Zealanders took part in the Somme operations, our Battalion was road making, sapping and repairing trenches. Shortly after the first two days our boys helped to push back the Germans. Several of our transport drivers were wounded and I was asked to join our transport, where I am now at the present time.

I remember the afternoon quite well, when our drivers were hit. I was washing some clothes about 400 yards away when I heard a roaring sound overhead. Knowing quite well what it was, I left my washing and bolted to the nearest safety sap some fifty yards away. I was only there a few seconds when the shell exploded and between 60 and 80 of our boys stampeded up to where I was. Some of them were lying asleep in our tents. Of course the explosion of the shell soon woke them up. After an interval of 20 minutes, waiting for more shells to land, we came out and I carried on with the washing. Others returned to the tents, only to find that some of our pals had been severely hit, two being killed outright, altogether, 11 casualties including 2 horses severely hit, 1 mule killed, 1 wagon badly damaged. The same evening I joined the transport.

After being on the Somme front for about six weeks we were

asked to leave for a well earned rest, facing another front. More quiet and not so much transport work to do, only harness cleaning and the usual daily transport routine.

On one occasion, before our departure from the Somme, I and another fellow were sent out to the trenches with 4 mules and the water cart, with water and extra rations for two of our Companies. After delivering our water and rations, when returning to our camp some 2 miles back, the Germans commenced to shell an artillery position alongside the track where we had to pass. As we neared this spot a shell dropped right alongside of us. Luckily for us the ground was soft as it had rained the night before. We were covered with mud. I got a smack on the left shoulder with a big lump of clay. I thought I was gone. My mate was worse off. He couldn't see in front of him for mud. Our mules were frightened as could be and bolted right back to camp. I was holding on for grim death.

The traffic police tried to stop us, but all in vain of course. Knowing quite well what startled the mules, they didn't mind so much. However, I was as much frightened, if not more, than the mules. I think if the ground was hard I am quite sure we would have been blown up to pieces. Well, that same shell killed four Tommies, one horse, and smashed up an ammunition limber so I think we were very lucky, don't you think?

I will write about how I spent Christmas day and New Year's Day next week. However, I do hope that you enjoyed yours immensely. Several light falls of snow occurred recently but nothing to write home about. At present we are having some very cold weather, very heavy frosts in the morning, followed by rain and cold winds during the day.

I have a very sore throat at present and can hardly speak. I went on sick parade twice, but they could do nothing as this has been the only time I have been on sick parade, since being over here. Now we have been here nearly nine months. I think I am standing it well. I have met several boys from down the old place. Fred Stretz, Len Palmer, Randall Harris, young Williams of Leeston, Redmond and only George Taiaroa I haven't met yet, but he was not very far away.

Dear Virgie, I thank you very much for your small packet of sweets, which arrived two days ago and I enjoyed them very much. I also received the three Christmas cards you all sent me. I am enclosing one with this letter for Granny, as I haven't sent her anything yet. How did the Boss like the card I sent him? Well Virgie, I will ring off with kind remembrance and arohanui.

A little more experience news next time.
Yours Sincerely Bill
France

The early months of 1917 were spent preparing for the Battle of Messines.[1] The Pioneer Battalion companies were organised along the following lines:

    A Company — Ngāpuhi and South Island
    B Company — Pākehā
    C Company — Bay of Plenty, Ngāti Porou, Hawke's Bay, Wairarapa
    D Company — Te Arawa, Waikato, Wellington, West Coast,
                     Whanganui, Taranaki

The weather continued to be damp and dull with a couple of falls of snow. Māori soldiers earned a reputation for being hard working, well organised and cheerful despite the conditions they faced. Their military skill and work ethic gained the respect of their fellow soldiers and commanders. Their efforts became instrumental in changing attitudes within New Zealand towards Māori. Despite their hard work, amid the seriousness of war, Māori solders also found opportunities for amusement.

2/1/17

Dear Virgie
I received today your letter written on the 29th Oct and the parcel of papers. I am greatly indebted to you for supplying me constantly with papers and it's always a treat to me to read the busters, but I regret to say that it was with great sadness when

I read of the loss Sedgemere has sustained through the death of Bertie McGill. I read his name in the casualty list, announcing him wounded, but I never knew that he has since died of wounds. Also Billy Simpson. The last time I met Bertie was in Egypt and the last time I met Simpson was in France here just before we left for the Somme Front.

However, one's life is not worth a farthing out here. I have had some narrow escapes myself out here. I have seen several horse columns getting blown up while taking ammunition and food supplies up to the firing line. It's an awful sight to see teams and men getting blown up. I will never forget these sights to my dying day.

I have not yet received the parcel sent out from old friends, however, I will never forget their generosity. I am pleased to know that I am out here doing a little for those at home.

I enjoyed Christmas day and dinner immensely. Roast pork, geese, beef and vegetables. Plum pudding and beer galore. I was pretty well stunned to beat the band as the saying is out here.

New Year's Eve we spent a rather enjoyable evening. Several of our boys went out to tin-can some of our officers. I was again slightly intoxicated so was unable to take part. I slept in full marching order that night, that is to say clothes, boots and everything. At any rate, next morning I woke up with a terrible big, swelled head. As there was a French Estaminet (or hotel) close by our stables, I soon got rid of that dry parch in the throat and was able to carry on with the day's duties. However, we were all a sorry looking lot of lads New Year's Day. After stables and an hour exercising our horses, we were given the rest of the day at our leisure, which we were greatly in need of.

Now that the New Year has passed, we have settled down to the usual daily routine once again. Football is practically compulsory out here for all our troops. The French people are only commencing to thresh their harvest. It seems quite a long time to leave in stacks since last August, which is their harvesting month. All their crops are stacked and thatched but the way they get their threshing done is quite out of date compared to our method in New Zealand. They also have more men, and a few women helping. The thresher is driven by an old Poelathe engine. They have now commenced to plough their land which is very slow work. Only one horse is used in the plough, single furrow. What we do in a single day, they do in a week.

The only thing that is passable, and that I have a good word for, is that their soldiers are good fighters and the French girls are not at all bad looking and very sociable girls to speak to.

Well, we are having some very cold and wet weather, but we are well provided with thick warm clothes, and compulsory bathing parades are essential. Whenever we are all taken for a bath we are given a clean change of clothes so we are not so badly off. But from what I hear the trenches are pretty wet just now. I am very pleased to say that I am not with the Company.

Daddy is at present in England, attending a course of infantry instruction prior to his return to New Zealand. I don't know whether he will return to the front again or he may be kept in New Zealand for the purpose of instructing recruits for the late reinforcements which will be a good job.

I was offered a chance to take a couple of stripes but I wouldn't take it. It's not worth it. I am doing alright where I am as driver. Especially as we are allowed one shilling extra. No responsibility on one's shoulders, if promoted an NCO. Well Virgie, I will now close these few lines. Hoping these may find you all well. These leave me the same.

Remembrance and arohanui.
Yours sincerely, friend, Bill.

The Finchams were among many families from the Taumutu, Sedgemere and Lakeside communities who sent parcels and newspapers to the local men who had gone to war. These gifts meant a great deal to the soldiers, who were so far away from home.

Somewhere in France
28/1/17

Dear Virgie

Please extend my heartfelt thanks to those kind ladies and gentlemen who had willingly subscribed towards the nice parcel I received a few days ago. Though far away from home and friends, the kindness Sedgemere and the vicinity has already shown will not be forgotten, and I only sincerely hope that the time and day will not be very long before I may have the personal privilege of returning my thanks for the kindness I have received since I have been abroad. I do hope and ask you to publicly thank one and all.

I am enjoying the very best of good health but it's awfully cold over here at present. There are hard fronts prevailing, and the snow has been lying now on the ground for some considerable time. We have had great sport snowballing but owing to the coldness we had to cut it right out. Football is all the craze here just now. Evening entertainments are well provided for the troops. Our Pioneers built a rather fine building for cinema and concert purposes and all the leading soldier artists, practically all New Zealanders, provide these entertainments. There is a first class orchestra and a troupe of singers called the Kiwis takes part. Enclosed please find the programme. I may mention the building is called the Kapai Theatre. All the latest songs, rag-time, sentimental, love songs and humorous are being sung in the very best style.

Also, the pictures are second to none, which is saying a lot, especially being so close behind the firing line.

How is the new hall? Has it been finished and opened? I am anxiously waiting to hear news concerning same. Please supply me with some at your earliest. Also, I wish to ask how are all the old folks at home? All keeping well I hope. Has uncle faced the music? I guess he will want to hurry along won't he. Otherwise you will be beating him badly.

I am very sorry to hear that your cousin has been wounded.

Please accept my deepest sympathy. I am hoping that he will soon recover. I regret that I had not the pleasure of meeting him out here. Probably I may have, who knows. Please accept this postcard as a token of friendship for old times' sake. Well now, the time is swiftly flying. Please excuse my abrupt conclusion, with kind remembrance and arohanui to all.

*Yours sincerely
Dvr. W.K. Maopo
France
PS parcel arrived in good condition.*

The harsh frosts made the Battalion's work difficult. Although the ground was frozen to around four inches thick, work continued on dugouts, drains, and roads. Eventually the ground began to thaw. The quiet monotony of the activities made the days pass more slowly, and thoughts of home crowded in.

'À L'Absent' postcard, front and back.
Author's collection

Somewhere in France
16/2/17

Dear Virgie

Things are awfully quiet at present. The snow which had been lying on the ground for three or four weeks is gradually melting away, and the weather is much warmer during the day, which is very much in our favour, for honestly speaking we have had some very cold weather, more than I'd like to go through again. The war doesn't seem to be getting nearer the finish since I left home, and I'm an old soldier now, at least I think so. We hear a lot of rumours that this spring will about see the finish of the war, but I've my doubts about it. That was the talk last spring and the war is still going strong.

I have to thank both Grandma and yourself for the two small parcels I received and the papers. I presume Miss Anderson sent some also. Please give her my best wishes and many thanks.

What's happened at home I wonder? I haven't heard from any of them for some considerable time now. I don't know whether my letters have gone astray, or whether they have forgotten me altogether. However I am almost in despair for the want of home news. I wrote home asking for an explanation.

I sincerely hope that you won't forget a fellow altogether. I suppose, ere this reaches you, Sergeant Major Pohio has arrived in New Zealand and has been along to visit his old friends. Whether he will return to the front again I don't know, it is to be hoped that we may have it all settled up before he is asked to return. Whether another big push will be made again or not, it's rather difficult to say, I hope so, and that the next time you hear from me we are somewhere in Germany or near Berlin. Of course it is very difficult to jump to conclusions so early in the year for what may take place inside six months.

Least I forget, I must tell you that every one of us has received two small gift boxes from the Auckland Patriotic Women's Committee. The first box I got contained a tin of cigarettes, 1 pr socks, a towel, 1 khaki pocket handkerchief, 1 tablet of chocolates, a picture post-card scenery from Auckland and also the donor's name and compliments. The second box consisted of two tins of cigarettes, 1 tin of lollies, 1 tin of luncheon, cheese, 1 tin of fish, 1 tin of sheep's tongue, tablets of chocolate and 1 tin of capstan pipe tobacco. Also the donor's name, address and compliments. So we are not doing so badly off. We are well supplied with pipe tobacco and cigarettes, issued every week.

Has the new hall been finished yet? I see by the New Zealand papers that a number of the young men who have not yet enlisted will soon be called up. So I guess you'll be soon losing your young man, if you don't watch him.

How is everybody at home? All well I hope. What was the harvest like this year? Did Uncle have a good threshing return? I daresay you would have had rather a busy time, during the harvest operations.

I heard from Johnnie Patterson, that he and the two boys were busy working the milking machines this season. He mentioned that the cows, generally speaking, were milking fairly well, so I guess the old farm must be paying some. The land here looks pretty good and the crops I've already seen convinced me that the land is worth its weight in gold, only for the severe winter. I wouldn't mind remaining over here after the war. However, I wouldn't mind another glimpse of old New Zealand after having been away nearly two years. Far too long for this child I think.

I was greatly amused at the system of farming over here. Single furrowed ploughs are used, which is far too slow for the New Zealand system. Last week I saw a threshing machine at work, close to our billets. Horses are used, drawing the plant from place to place. Poelathe engines. The combine is a lot smaller than those in New Zealand. No elevators used. Only two bags can be hung up for the grain but the most amusing part of all was that all the straw passing through the rear position is gathered up by an apparatus after the same system as on the reaper and binder used for gathering and tying bundles, and ties the straw up exactly the same as the reaper and binder.

The French people stack all their straw and what is not stacked outside is castered into big lofts, where it is kept dry for chaff for winter feeding. I might mention the straw here is very long and practically clean. The oats straw makes lovely chaff. We are using a lot for chaff which we cut ourselves with a small hand chaff cutter. The threshing operations are very slow and more hands are employed than used on the threshers in New Zealand. Fourteen men I counted on the mill I saw. Anyone should make wages if paid by the hour. The farm horses used are really beautiful beasts. Fine, big, upstanding lean legged and plenty of action, all driven with one rein and are so very quiet too.

Well Virgie I must really bring this to a close, as time is limited, army candle issue scarce and lastly news absolutely exhausted. Hoping you are all well, as these leave me at present, with kind remembrance and arohanui,

Yours sincerely
Friend Bill

9

Letters from home

The letters from home were a lifeline for soldiers fighting so far away from family and friends. The men eagerly awaited news from home, especially during the winter months. For Wiremu, preparations were under way for the Battalion to move north, to Messines.

> Somewhere in France
> 9/4/17
>
> Dear Virgie
> After a relapse of two or three months waiting patiently for home and local news without receiving same, I decided to write and say that I am keeping well and managed to pull through the cold weather and snow without any serious colds, which I was very thankful for considering the very rough and severe winter we had to contend with.
> We are now having foggy and fair weather, not quite so cold. We have just lately taken up new quarters after a long spell of 4 or 5 months in winter quarters, which was like real home after a few weeks of strenuous hardships on the western front.
> Our present quarters are not so up-to-date, especially the transport billets, which is an ordinary loft or straw barn. However, we are making the rough conditions the best way possible, hoping it will be only for a short while.

I don't think the war will last much longer. I do believe at the end of six months will see things quite normal again as we are slowly and gradually wearing the Germans down. I also think that another big advance and heavy gun bombardment will finish the Huns. Generally speaking the Germans and their allies are retreating before our heavy guns on all fronts. Our Pioneers are pretty well scattered all over France. I am still with our Transport, driving at present. We are having rather a good time, hardly any carting to do excepting for cleaning and shining our harness. We would have nothing to do, other than exercising our horses and mules which is absolutely compulsory.

I am pleased to say that the people where we are now billeted are very sociable and nearly all speak and understand English pretty well and we get along splendidly. The civilians charge very dearly for anything they sell to us. We pay for eggs, threepence half penny each, sugar ten pence a pound, French bread ten pence, French beer a penny a glass, which is the only cheap stuff on sale to be bought. I suppose everything is very dear in New Zealand in present which must be very unpleasant. The farmers over here are busy putting their ground in order for sowing. Some have already commenced to sow their grain, a few paddocks have been sown and is just coming through above the ground and looking well.

The farming system is a long way behind our system. The other morning while exercising I saw a fellow drilling oats. The drill used is only a small apparatus with a small box not much larger than a big candle box or case for the grain, with three coulters drawn by one horse. Another thing I noticed was that the ground is roughly worked prior to the grain being sown. A light set of wooden harrows is put over the ploughing, which only scratches the top of the ridge before the sowing.

The land too is absolutely first class, much better than a lot of the best in New Zealand. I have seen the soil down to nearly six foot without any sign of that hard clay which is well known in our district, only three or four inches to a foot deep. Quite a lot of stable manure is used, in fact all the manure used is stable manure. Altogether, give me the good New Zealand system of farming. Done!

Well, Virgie how is everybody keeping at home? All well I hope. I am very pleased to receive the Auckland Weekly news today you sent me. Thanks very much. I hope you have received the small handkerchief box I sent along with Mrs Cant's. I think it's the least that I could do, was to send something along after receiving such a lot of papers and sundries from you.

I notice that quite a lot of our boys from our district are being called up to enlist so I am pleased to know that our district is well represented out here. Well, as time is getting on I must bring this to a close. Hoping this will find you enjoying the best of health as this leaves me the same.

Best wishes and arohanui to all.
Sincerely yours
W.K. Maopo

As the New Zealanders continued to prepare for the attack on Messines, Wiremu caught up with one of his old friends from Taumutu and received the welcome news that his sister Hinewai had given birth to a daughter, whom she had named Edna Huirapa Cant. Wiremu knew Hinewai and her husband Len would be overjoyed. He too celebrated the arrival of the newest family member.

Somewhere in France
16/4/17

Dear Virgie
I have again taken the liberty of writing a few hurried lines to say that I am well and sorry to hear that the old farm has been auctioned which I heard last month. Also, I heard that the 'Boss' has at last done the trick of marrying Jessie, which was only expected after such a long time courting.

Where are you and Grandma living now? Please forward me your new address will you. Where are the Pattersons? Who are the new owners of Willow Glen at present? I am writing this to your old address trusting it will reach you alright.

I see in papers that several men and young boys have been called up by ballot. I saw George Lochhead's name amongst the list. Poor George would do it pretty hard for the training is fairly severe. However, he'll wish he was still on the farm. I do wish the war will soon be finished before he's ready to embark from New Zealand, for I think 'ere this reaches you we will be going strong on our way to 'Berlin', singing 'We are the boys of the old Brigade'.

A few days ago I had the pleasure of meeting George Taiaroa. He looks well. Oh you should have seen us laughing and talking of old times. One would think that no war was in progress. Only for the booming of guns and the whirring of planes above us, which soon reminded us of our position. However we were both pleased of each other's strange meeting over here.

We were distributed with small parcels last week from New Zealand. I received one from Mrs Scott of Brookside containing socks, cake and sweets, also a note wishing the lucky recipient the best of good luck and wishes. I have sent back her card of acknowledgement.

I hope you received the small parcel I sent along. I am expecting a small parcel from Hinewai. She wrote and told me to that effect. I have also received some papers you sent, which I have to thank you very much for. The busters were very interesting. All the more so being chiefly home news.

So, the new hall has at last been completed and officially opened, and what a turn out you must have had. What a time we poor beggars missed, eh? I can imagine the good time the boys were having waltzing around while we boys are doing it hard over here. What luck some fellows have.

Well Virgie, I am running out of news to say for the present. So I will now conclude with my best wishes and arohanui.

Kind remembrance to Grandma

Yours sincerely
Bill

◆ The Last *Maopo*

Māori soldiers eating lunch in the trenches.
Auckland War Memorial Museum Tamaki Paenga Hira, Photograph H 468 D530

In April the Pioneer companies continued a regime of regular construction, digging and tunnelling, although the work was made easier by the improving weather. Wiremu left the transport and was sent back to join his company after an over-exuberant case of celebration, having now survived for one full year amid the battlefields. When the farm was put up for sale, Virgie prepared to leave Taumutu with Granny.

> *Bill*
> *Somewhere in Belgium*
> *19/5/17*
>
> *Dear Virgie*
> *I was so pleased to hear from you that I am hastening to reply right away. I only posted a letter to you last night. I thank you very much for your kindness in sending me the pretty handkerchief. You can bet your life it won't be my fault if I lose it. So don't be*

surprised to see it with me when I have the good fortune to be one of the lucky boys to return home. I have put it well south in my little kit valise.

Thanks awfully for sending along the cutting from the buster of the opening ceremonies of the new hall, which was very interesting. I don't mind telling you that I was very pleased when reading the opening account. I felt as if I was there also. You guess my mind imagined a great deal just on the spur of the moment.

Oh, you should have seen my face when I read of your complimentary remarks concerning my little niece. I sincerely hope that you were not overdoing it. However, I hope to have the pleasure of nursing her and keeping her out of mischief. She should be able to speak a little when I return.

Well Virgie, I regret to hear that the old farm has been put up, also that you and Grandma will be leaving old Taumutu. I am sure everybody will be very sorry to see you all leaving them. I too will miss you all when I return. I am sure I will miss those jokes and sayings we all used to crack together, however only time will heal up our aching hearts. Whatever happens, I won't forget to pay you and Grandma a flying visit whenever I have the opportunity, if I won't be trespassing. (I don't think, eh.) Poor old Grandma will feel it very much won't she.

No doubt quite a lot of changes have taken place since I left home. I felt sorry when I read your letter to that effect. Never mind, we are winning over here and that's one good consolation. As regards Daddy being behind with his replies, he has been away from us for some considerable time. Yes, the papers find me alright.

But what do you think, I have left the transport. You know that it's just past 12 months ago this month since we have been over here, so several of us young bloods were celebrating the event to our heart's content. Consequently some of us overstepped the mark so had to beat a hasty retreat to our respective Companies. So please use my old address in future. The defence department is drafting out the shirkers.

The Last *Maopo*

I am still awaiting my leave to 'Blighty' as London is named over here. All leave has been again indefinitely suspended, awaiting another big move so we are told. So I am again unlucky missing a trip of a lifetime especially this time of the year. Now that summer is fast approaching, everything is looking at its loveliest. I have not had too much of the French girls. I have not had time whatever for any of them. Although, I have seen some of the finest and prettiest looking girls I have ever seen so far. But I would not turn down our own, it would be rather mean, wouldn't it.

Well Virgie, I have no more news to write about for the present. Hoping you are all enjoying the best of health, as this leaves me at present. So I will conclude with best wishes and arohanui and kia ora koe.

Sincerely yours, kind remembrance to all.
Bill

10

Wiremu visits 'Blighty'

By June the troops were under a constant barrage of gunfire as they were embroiled in the Battle of Messines. Constructing tramlines and digging communication trenches under heavy fire, the Pioneers suffered increased casualties. The Battalion lost 17 men, and a further 133 were wounded or gassed. Wiremu's health began to suffer and he had a brief spell in the army hospital.

Wiremu received the news that Willow Glen had been sold at auction. It was sold in blocks, to three different buyers. Herb Fincham purchased a new farm property called The Peaks, near Hawarden. Granny and Virgie moved to Stratford Street in Christchurch.

Willow Glen Homestead, Fincham Farm.
Photograph supplied by Joan Overhill

The Last *Maopo*

Belgium
5/6/17

Dear Virgie

It is with great regret I read of the account of the old farm having been sold. Also of the great clearing sale the Master had, which I had been duly notified of from home, as well as the farewell social and presentation to the Willow Glen household. I read the report in the Weekly Press. I can assure you no one ever felt more sorry than I to hear that the old farm has changed hands. I hear a Mr Brown has bought Willow Glen, has he not?

Really, you must excuse me if I am behind with my correspondence for I have been away in the Hospital sick, and only rejoined my unit a short time ago, and as we were pretty busy I hadn't very much time to write any earlier, so I am hurrying along to catch the early outgoing mail.

I am now enjoying the best of good health. Hoping soon to help give Fritz another deadly blow and so help to bring this awful long struggle to a peaceful end for all time. I think you will hear me out in saying that with ordinary luck I won't be back home for three, perhaps five years' time as I already wrote and told you before. However I hope I'm very much out of my reckoning, 'eh what?'

Please don't forget to write and let me know where you are located at present. I can hardly write for the noise and din of the guns outside our dugouts. Our guns have started to strafe the enemy trenches. Guns of all sizes and calibres are taking part all around us. An hour ago Fritz woke up and sent a few shells over to us, killing one of our boys and wounding three others. The one killed belonged to the same platoon as me. A shell caught him fair in the body, killing him instantaneously. One boy got a leg broken, the others were only slight wounds. Oh, I have seen some very pitiful sights out here. So you can imagine, one must really have very strong nerves to withstand everything that goes on nearly every day of the week. Matter of fact, it's only one's luck that pulls him through without being hit.

Well Virgie, only fancy the Master sent along a portion of their wedding cake for me. I think it's rather kind of them to think of me. It came as a surprise too. Never for a moment did I ever think of tasting such luxury out in France. I must write and thank them for their kindness. So please hurry along and do likewise so that I may have another chance to partake a portion of yours also. Of course I am only joking you know.

Our present surrounding is just a picture of loveliness. Spring is at hand, all fruit trees are in full bloom, crops behind the lines looking grand and forest trees looking their very best. Only for the boom and dull thud of big guns and falling shells, one would really think he was at home. At present our big guns have just opened again. We can hardly hear each other for the noise from the reports and the screeching shells as they hurry over head to the German lines whilst yours truly is well down in the old dugout, expecting Fritz to retaliate.

I have a German shellcase ring in possession. I am keeping it to send you as a souvenir. It would make two serviette rings, which look lovely when polished. I am also trying to get two for Hinewai. As it is very difficult to send them away directly from here, I would wait until someone goes to England on Furlough, where better chances are available for dispatching them away. Orders have been issued some time ago authorizing all troops that no such articles as shell casing rings, helmet etc are allowed to be sent away from France. Though of course if such articles could only be safely carried across to England, well the rest is quite manageable. I know of several boys who sent such things from England. I daresay you have seen pictures in the New Zealand Weekly papers of them, where relatives and friends have received them from the front.

Well Virgie, I will now conclude as tea is right ready, and to delay is to go without. Our motto is fall in and follow me.

Hoping you are all keeping well.
Kind remembrance and arohanui
Yours sincerely
Friend Bill.

♥ The Last *Maopo*

A welcome respite came at the end of June, when Wiremu was granted leave in England. He was able to take in the sights of England and Scotland, and take reprieve from the battlefields.

> New Zealand Soldiers Club
> 17,18,23 Russell Square
> W.C
> July 6-7 1917
>
> Dear Virgie
> Just a few lines to say that I am keeping well and have had quite an enjoyable time over here on leave now. I have only two more days to go then I shall have to make shift back over to France, jove, after the good time I had too. Oh, 'Blighty' is the place for me. I couldn't manage to visit any stud farms as time was limited, and the farms are a long way to the North of Edinburgh. However, may have the chance next year if I'm lucky enough.
> Well Virg. I had the time of my life, it really opened my eyes when I saw Blighty for the first time, 'some place' as the saying goes out here. I was taken out by a guide the day after I arrived to see the wonders of the place. Some of us boys on leave were driven out to the Tower of London, London Bridge, Houses of Parliament, Westminster Abbey, St Paul's Cathedral, Albert Hall and Albert Monument through Hyde Park, right past the King's Palace, better known as Buckingham Palace. I also saw the largest clock in London, Big Ben, and I saw all the most fashionable houses in Park Lane. 'Gad' I saw some very pretty places, Leicester Square, Piccadilly, the Pall Mall, all the New Zealand Banks offices. Altogether I had rather a very interesting time.
> The same applied too when I went to Scotland. I visited the Forth Bridge and went aboard the Warships Australia and Sydney. The New Zealand was in also, but no visitors were allowed to go on her as she was getting ready to enter the docks for repairs.
> Edinburgh Castle is a sight worth seeing, also Princess Street, the prettiest in Scotland. One side of Princess Street is all the big

buildings, on the other side are botanic gardens and statues of the greatest men of their days in Scotland and various other lovely parks well laid out. Of course, being summer out here things were looking very good indeed really.

I can hardly think of what to write and where to start and I suppose this is from seeing too much at once. No doubt on account of the war, I saw more girls in Edinburgh and London than I ever saw in all my life, of course these are very large towns. However, after all, I wish I was back in old New Zealand.

Well Virg, excuse my scribbling as I am in a hurry to meet a chap, we are going to the theatre. I am returning to France in two days' time and will write again when I arrive back to my unit. How are you and Granny keeping, quite well I hope? Please write and give me your address, as I am writing to your old address at present. Thank you very much for sending me the Weekly Press which arrives pretty regular.

I have heard that George Taiaroa was killed out here and Fred Stretz was reported wounded. No doubt you saw it in the papers. Poor George. Fancy, I was with him and Fred and H. Rapley 3 or 4 days before we went out to take Messines. You remember Tom Brown, who used to live at Mrs Pucks? He got wounded too, also Joe Barlow from Little River.

Well Virgie, I must now say goodbye and remember me to Granny. Hoping you are both well.

Arohanui, from sincerely friend Bill.

Leave came to an end and Wiremu returned to his battalion, which was now in Flanders, Belgium. He continued working on building dugouts and burying cables for the French artillery.

Lieutenant Colonel King noted that the men were becoming more proficient in the French language: 'Our boys are getting very friendly with the other troops around here and their language is getting more mixed every day. It's quite a common thing to hear a man use three or four languages in the one sentence at any time, and now it's getting worse.'[1]

The Last *Maopo*

His father's traditional karakia still afforded Wiremu protection against the dangers of war, while many of his comrades were succumbing to injury. He endured many heavy shelling episodes without being hit.

> In the Field
> 20-7-17
>
> Dear Virgie
> Thank you very much for the beautiful card you sent me and the result of Daddy's social and presentation, which I received this afternoon. Having nothing to do, I thought it best to reply straight away. You must excuse the smallness of writing paper this time, as I mislaid my writing tablet. As nearly everyone is busy writing letters, I had to carry on with what spare papers I had.
> Yes, Granny's pair of socks arrived with the Xmas parcel safely. The box of chocolates you sent along arrived in good condition after I was away on leave, but I saw none of it. One of our boys claimed it all. Of course he told me what he did with them, so I said nothing as he had shared them with our other boys.
> Yes, I was very interested in the social welcome to Daddy. No doubt you must have all been pleased to see him once more. I don't think I will ever return until we have deservedly beaten the Germans for all time, I left New Zealand with that thought mingled through my mind, even if it takes another two or three years to defeat them. They are slowly and surely being driven back to their own country.
> We are expecting to go into action again very soon. 'Ere this reaches you, we may be going at it hammer and tongs for our very lives, and I hope to come out again without a scratch, for I have been very lucky indeed so far, being in the heaviest right throughout at Messines without a shell. However, we are all getting very tired of it, and hoping it to come to a finish soon.
> You might have remembered a while ago I promised that I would get my Pioneer Badge embroidered and send you one.

Well I am unable to fulfil my promise but I am sending you the real badge, a spare one I have, with a German shell casing ring, one I got while at the Somme. The ring would make, if cut, good serviette rings. The Badge is off my hat, a large one, it was the first one issued to me. I have carried it with me fully twelve months so I hope you would like it.

Well Virgie, I am sending enclosed a Postcard of a pet dog cemetery I had visited while in London. You will notice that the dogs are buried in decent little graves with tombstones erected to their memory. Of course this is only a small portion of the cemetery you see here. The whole area must be fully two acres, a caretaker lives right close by where I got this Postcard from.

I must now close with arohanui to you both.
From your friend Bill.
I am quite well.

Te Hokowhitu a Tū badge with NZNC (NZ Native Contingent) at the base of the badge, although the official title was NZ Māori Contingent.

Photograph and explanation supplied by Brent Nunns

New Zealand Pioneers badge. In February 1916 the New Zealand forces were reorganised after the Gallipoli campaign. The New Zealand Māori Contingent were used to form part of the New Zealand Pioneer Battalion, and they were issued the second pattern badge with 'Pioneers' in the bottom scroll. In September 1917 the New Zealand Pioneer Battalion, as promised by General Godley, became an all-Māori unit. It was reformed as the New Zealand Māori Pioneer Battalion and was issued with the badge that features the initials 'NZ' at the base.

Photograph and explanation supplied by Brent Nunns

11

Changes at home

Two years after Wiremu's departure, many things had changed in Taumutu. Various families had sold their farms and moved away. Having sons and husbands at war and receiving regular reports of local soldiers being killed or wounded had a big impact on the small community.

Phoebe's sister, Emma, had not settled at Taumutu, and in July 1917 Fred and Emma sold the farm and moved back to the North Island, where Fred purchased a dairy farm at Oparure, near Te Kuiti. The local Taumutu community held a farewell service for the family. The event was noted in the local paper:

> *Mr and Mrs F. Schnelle and family, who are leaving to reside in the North Island, were entertained at a well-attended social gathering in the Sedgemere Hall on Thursday evening, and were presented with a silver tea service. Mr J.T. Parkin presided. Mr T.B. Howson, in making the presentation, said that Mr Schnelle's parents had settled in Sedgemere fifty years ago when there were no roads and the district was practically undrained swamp. The family had been neighbours of his for forty years, and he was sorry that the district was losing such worthy residents as Mr and Mrs F. Schnelle.*

In France, the month of August was wet and the trenches were a mess. The troops were now assisting with the work in Flanders.[1]

❧ The Last *Maopo*

Headquarters, A Company and D Company had to be relocated as they were shelled in the middle of the night.

> In the field
> 1st/8/1917
>
> Dear Virgie
> Just a few hurried lines to let you know that I am still indulging with the best of health, after a very good holiday behind the lines, consisting of 10 days. Our unit was ordered up close to the lines and I can assure you I don't half care for the idea of being up so close. The Germans, ever since we arrived to our camp area, have been mighty busy with their heavy guns.
> The fourth night we were here, somewhere between ten and twelve o'clock, everybody was roused out by the thundering noise of exploding shells right alongside our camp. Oh, you should have seen us running in all directions to take cover, nearly everyone with practically next to nothing on in the way of clothing. Myself, I had only my trousers and boots on when I left the camp. Luckily for us only a few shells landed around us, otherwise the boys would have had to sleep out in the open, and being a chilly night, things would have been very unpleasant.
> After nearly an hour away we returned to camp, but all hands could not sleep, expecting more shells over. None came, and excepting for loss of sleep we fared very well, escaping without any casualties. Early morning brought us great relief. Only two platoons were detailed off for duty to proceed to work in the trenches. As the platoon I'm in was one for duty I had to go, however, having completed our day's work we moved out to return to camp. On our way we were met with a heavy rainstorm, drenching us completely. As we had no dry change of clothes, you can imagine the unpleasantness we were put to. Only for our greatcoats, I believe I would have suffered very badly.
> To make matters worse, during the night we were again turned out of our cosy camp by more shells, but this time they landed right in the midst of our camp, killing one fellow instantaneously.

How we escaped without further casualties is a serious mystery to us all. I will not forget it as long as I live, I tell you. I got away very quickly with only a shirt on and a pair of socks. As there was a light falling rain at the time, we got the worst of it again. I might mention to further our troubles we had to proceed in the dark through a paddock full of growing Californian thistles, up to our knees in height. So, you can fully imagine we were having a time. We returned to camp when the shelling was over. We took away our rifles and belongings and made the best of it in some other old dugouts previously used by other troops, out of shell range for the night. Next morning we got orders to remove our camp and up to the time of writing we have enjoyed peace and quietness.

I have no more to say for the present, for this will really tire you to death. Of course this is only a few of several happenings. What the soldier has to put up with out here! But we are told that Fritz is getting more than his own share back just now.

The weather is simply rotten just now, raining cats and dogs, making it very miserable for the boys. Dear Virgie, thank you for saying that you are making me a pair of socks. I'm sure it will come in very handy. I haven't heard from Hinewai for fully eight months. If it hadn't been for you writing so often my mail would be practically nil. Hoping both you and Granny are well. I will be very pleased to hear from you again.

Sincere regards and arohanui until we meet again.
Your sincere friend Bill
Tell Granny I'm always wondering how she is.

The cold, wet weather continued through August. At night the wiring parties went out to construct wire entanglements and, during these episodes, they incurred heavy casualties. It rained continuously and the enemy artillery fire was relentless. The Māori soldiers had a rough time, but most of the wire entanglements were constructed successfully in spite of the conditions. Each day of work they saw more of their comrades fall in the battles of Messines. This was perhaps the most grim period so far.

♥ The Last *Maopo*

Māori soldiers give a haka at the New Zealand Division boxing championships in Doulieu, France, during the First World War.
Royal New Zealand Returned and Services' Association: New Zealand official negatives, World War 1914–1918. Alexander Turnbull Library, Wellington, New Zealand, Ref. 1/2-012840-G

In the Field
16-8-17

Dear Virgie

Since I wrote last we have been having some awful weather, raining every other day or night, making life very miserable for us out here. The trenches are nothing but a mass of sticky mud and water, over waist deep in places, and it is very difficult to walk up and down the saps without stumbling over a sunken sandbag or other wooden material hidden under the mud. Every day after returning to camp from trench repairing and other work connected with our daily routine, we are covered from waist to foot with mud. Of course, having only one change of clothing, we had to turn to and do a little washing, the most difficult part was the drying process. If our clothes weren't properly dry they were put on and we had to carry on getting ready to go out again, only to get wet once more, so you can imagine what a treat we are having. But now that we are getting quite used to this sort of thing we don't mind a bit.

Thank you very much for the two papers you sent along. I also received several daily papers a few days ago from Miss Anderson (Sedgemere School). A New Zealand mail is expected in at any time now, and I am expecting quite a number of letters this time. I am hoping to get some from Hinewai and Len. I wrote to them asking for an explanation, however, if I don't hear from them this coming mail I will have to give up writing to them altogether. You couldn't blame me, eh?

I am expecting to get away on furlough again, some time about Christmas if I'm lucky. You will notice by the papers that our Battalion has been losing heavy casualties lately. Our company in four days lost three officers killed. Another company has lost one officer and another was severely wounded. Several new drafts have joined us and a number of them have again left, being either killed or wounded. One young fellow joined one evening, and the next morning he proceeded out to the trenches, but was only in there an hour when he was killed by a shell. This is nearly an everyday occurrence out here.

I met Reg Thian and George Harper last week. They are both looking well and looking forward to trying conclusions with the wiry German. As all our units are so widely scattered, we have very little chance of meeting each other, only by mere accident and unexpectedly.

There are a lot of other boys I know over here that I have been trying to find but couldn't, not knowing what company and unit they are with, so will only have to wait until we meet.

I would have liked to describe my adventures out in the trenches one night a fortnight ago, when I was sent out to put up a wire entanglement between our lines and the Germans when we were only about thirty yards away from them. Only I'm afraid that it would not pass the censoring people so I must pass it off.

In all probability I may have a new address when you hear

from me again as we are expecting to reorganise our companies shortly, but I will write and give my new address all the same if I have any. Hoping you are both well as I am at present.

Kia ora and arohanui to you both.
Yours sincerely
Friend Bill.

PS Please find enclosed two small pieces of Scotch Heather given to me while over in Scotland.

As a reprieve from the harshness of his present reality at Messines, Wiremu continued to write to his friend and reminisce about his time working on her family farm, recalling how the family teased him about his relationship with Phoebe Prentice.

In the Field
18-8-17

Dear Virgie
Your most welcome letter to hand this afternoon. I was pleased to hear that you have received the small parcel I sent along containing handkerchief box. I was wondering whether it had arrived as I haven't heard from you concerning same. I really thought that it had gone astray. However, I am glad it has reached its destination quite safely.
These small articles cost very little out here and it is quite a pleasure to me to purchase them and send them along for old friendship's sake. I have sent my hat badge and shell casing ring as curios and hope that you will get them safely too.
So you and Granny are not taking too kindly to town life, eh? I am sure it must be rather hard for Granny as she has been used to the country practically all her life. Really, I don't think I will miss coming to town to pay you and Granny a short visit when I do return. You know things are so uncertain out here, and one never knows when he is called up to answer the roll call over

yonder. However, I will always look forward cheerfully to the time when peace is declared.

So, you do believe that Granny's heart has softened. Do I remember those old days when I used to be growled at for cackling at the dining table, not I? They were the times! Often when lying in my little grey home in the west my thoughts used to wander back to those old times, especially too when she used to mention Phoebe Prentice's name and I used to deny it before her and didn't she used to barrack me, eh? Oh, many a laugh I have had out here, and again when reading your interesting letter. Tell her for me that I still cackle yet over old days. So it would be quite a treat renewing old friendships once more.

Granny Fincham.
Photograph supplied by Joan Overhill

I regret to mention that poor George Taiaroa was killed in action during the last advance over here that we took part in. Also Rapley and Randal Harris died of wounds. Fred Stretz was wounded, and is at present recuperating in England. I never knew George was killed until I was over on furlough and saw the casualty list over there posted up in the 'New Zealand Soldiers Club' for the boys over from France, some place too, I guess. It's very sad news, old Mrs Taiaroa would feel it very keenly. Moreso than the others I think, for he was her favourite. Strange, the last time I was speaking to him and Fred Stretz was 3 or 4 days before we went into action, and we were discussing the coming battle too. George was saying that he would give Fritz a lively time of it, he was a machine gunner. So you could imagine the shock I got when I saw his name amongst those brave boys who were killed.

Well, Virgie, I think you did very well giving me so much news about Taumutu, considering you are away. So Lakeside is building a new hall. I'm pleased that our wee corner took the lead and they followed suit. I thought somehow Sedgemere would beat them. No doubt quite a number of changes are taking place around Sedgemere since I left.

That reminds me that on the 18th of September next will be the second year since I said farewell to Taumutu and friends. Quite an old soldier now, ain't I just! I was thinking of celebrating the occasion with a few beers, if I'm lucky and holding only two bob a day you know, is not much to carry on with, is it. The beer is very much inferior to the New Zealand beer, over here and very much cheaper. Champagne is very cheap too but a very good drink to take.

The weather is just lovely at present, after a spell of wet weather extending over 7 or 8 days. The French people have commenced harvesting. The crops look remarkably well, but I don't like the way they gather and cut the crops. Mostly scythe is used for cutting, and tied in sheaves by hand. Altogether their method is a long way behind our New Zealand system. But above all I am dreading this coming winter. I had quite sufficient last year.

Well Virgie, I haven't any more news at present, so you must excuse me this time. Hoping you are both keeping well at home as this leaves me at present.

Kind regards to Granny and Emily.

Enclosed a few lines of arohanui to Emily.
Kia ora and arohanui
Yours sincerely
Friend Bill

At the end of August the Pākehā company within the Pioneers was drafted out. There were now enough Māori reinforcements to form a full Māori battalion. Once again, the Battalion adopted the name The New Zealand Māori Pioneer Battalion and the soldiers wore the Te Hokowhitu a Tū badge.

In the Field
26-8-17

Dear Virgie
I have the pleasure of acknowledging the receipt of your small parcel this afternoon containing 1 pair of socks, 1 packet cigarettes, 1 cake of soap and a tin case of coffee, sugar and milk tablets, which I thank you and Granny for very much. It's awfully kind of you both. My mates couldn't be convinced for some time that the socks were hand knitted, being so completely made, and I am keeping them until the cold winter sets in before I wear them, such a lovely fit too.
I am trying some of Granny's coffee tablets this evening at supper. I and my section mates have just finished having a real old meal of new potatoes, which we have pinched from a Frenchman's potato field when returning from our work. It is rumoured here that the South Island Maoris are sending over about 8,000 muttonbirds for the use of the Maori boys over here so you bet your life we are looking forward to a great tangi [hāngi].

We are having lovely weather just now and there is nothing much doing over here since last June when we gave Fritz another severe hiding, which cost us a lot of casualties of which you have already read in the paper. Our Pioneers lost very heavily this year, far more than ever we have had since we were made Pioneers.

Fancy, I got a letter from Len Cant yesterday. He tells me that he intends in future to write regularly every fortnight so I hope he will keep to his promise. He didn't forget to tell me that my young niece is doing splendidly and that I will be very proud of her.

I forgot to thank you in my letter last week for sending my old Pal Charlie Luinney's photo. Poor old boy. We spent some rare old times together when working at Emily's father's place at Lakeside. I wondered what became of him.

Also, the result of the clearing sale held at Willow Glen last autumn. It must have been a real tip top sale. I was awfully disgusted at the low prices the horses fetched. Did the Boss keep any of the draughts for himself? Who bought old Gladys, as I didn't see her name among those sold?

I see in the papers that a flying school has been started at Sockburn so you will see aeroplanes flying about galore very soon. Over here is the place for planes. I see air flights nearly every day.

While I was on leave I sent some Postcards from Edinburgh. Have you got them yet?

Please Virgie, will you thank the Boss and Jess for me for their kindness sending along a portion of their cake as I don't know where to write and thank them personally.

Well I hope you are both keeping well at home as I am at present.

Best wishes and arohanui
From yours sincere Bill
Remember me to Emily.

As he was writing to Virgie about receiving news from Len Cant, Wiremu was unaware that his young niece, Edna, Len and Hinewai's daughter, had just died at 12 months of age. The Maopo family had suffered another terrible loss. Hinewai did not have any other children.

In September Wiremu was appointed to Lance Corporal and the Battalion was on the move again, leaving Messines for war-battered Ypres to prepare for the Passchendaele offensive. B Company camped west of the town and south of the Poperinghe Road. On 4 October 1917, the New Zealand Division's guns opened fire on the German defences. Those who heard the artillery fire say it was the heaviest of the war and the Division took over a thousand prisoners.[2]

The wet weather turned the ground into a quagmire. Guns and horses became bogged down everywhere and the roads were in terrible condition. Many of the New Zealand Division's guns became bogged in mud on the road and never reached action.

This highlighted the vital importance of the labouring work the Māori soldiers did in pushing roads, light railways and tramlines forward to provide for advancements. When the Battalion ran short of supplies the transport lines were unable to be completed, and so the work done to their stopping point was rendered useless. This had a significant impact on the attacking ability of the New Zealand Division. The Pioneers attributed the failure of subsequent attacks to the lack of materials.[3]

Commanding Officer Lieutenant Colonel George Augustus King was killed at Passchendaele when the New Zealand Division was attacked. He was laid to rest at Ypres and farewelled by the Māori Battalion who had served with him. A witness at the service recounted, 'I do not think I will ever forget that service, a cloudless sky and an aeroplane scrap overhead, the shallow grave, the body strewn in a blanket and covered with the New Zealand flag, the surpliced Padre, the short impressive burial service and finishing up with a beautiful Maori lament for a fallen chief, *Piko nei te Matenga*, [*When our Heads are Bowed with Woe*] sung by the Maoris present, and with its beautiful harmonies and perfect tune, it seemed to me the most feeling tribute they could offer.'[4]

❦ The Last *Maopo*

Funeral of Lieutenant Colonel George Augustus King at Ypres during the First World War.

Royal New Zealand Returned and Services' Association: New Zealand official negatives, World War 1914–1918. Alexander Turnbull Library, Wellington, New Zealand, Ref. 1/2-012984-G

> No.6 Platoon, B.Coy, N.Z. Pioneers,
> N.Z.E.7
> Cl- GPO
> Wellington
> France
> Oct 31st 1917
>
> Dear Virgie
> Your most welcome letter of Aug 7th to hand. And I can assure you I was very pleased to hear from you. I really thought as I hadn't heard from you for some considerable time that you had forgotten me. However, I am pleased to know that I am still in your thoughts. Tell Granny that I am sorry that she had the misfortune to burn the pie and that she is not to get excited again over my letters. All the same, I would have given anything to partake of some.

Oh, what a lot of local news you gave me in your last letter. What a shame it rained that day the Lakeside Memorial Hall was opened. I'm sure it must have spoilt your day's outing. So altogether it was a lovely turnout. I guess the Lakeside Hall must be 'Some Hall', eh. No, I don't think that we will ever see any shops around Lakeside. Mr Schnelle must be overdoing it when he told the public that in his speech. At any rate, Lakeside must be very proud of their new hall, but I'm pleased Sedgemere got ahead of Lakeside with a new hall. Fancy us boys missing all the fun at home. But never mind, there's a good time coming for the boys.

We are having awful wet and cold weather over here just now. Quite a number of us are suffering with colds. I have got an awful sore head at present. However, I will endeavour to finish this letter before it gets worse.

Daddy has rejoined our Battalion, but he is not with our Company. He is attached to another Company at present. He is looking well. The trip home and back have made great improvement on him. I haven't spoken to him yet, as he hasn't been to see any of us yet, but I've seen him often on parade.

You will see by the Sept–Oct papers that we have been giving Fritz another death knock at Ypres. Our Infantry lost very heavily. Our own Battalion had very few casualties this time. I had some very narrow shaves from being hit but I must be rather a bad one to hit. Perhaps old 'Davey Jones' doesn't want me yet. I have received all the parcels you sent except the canteen. I daresay it will turn up alright. Oh, I must say that I have already worn out the pair of socks you sent me. As socks were very scarce at the time, I had to wear them. I thought I wouldn't want to wear them until the winter had properly set in. I hope you received the cuckoo feather I sent along, also scotch heathers.

So it was you that sent Jessie's cake along, was it? How thoughtful of you doing so. Yes, I received it in good condition. Two days ago some muttonbirds arrived and we had rather an excellent breakfast and dinner. The best two meals we have had for a long time. I intend to turn over a new leaf next year and try to be *good. I'm afraid these celebrations will be my downfall, if I don't take a pull.*

I received a letter from Jock Patterson a few days ago, informing me that my little niece Edna is dead. She died on the 14th of Aug last. Poor wee kiddie, I feel so sorry. Hinewai did write and tell me that Edna wasn't too well, but I never dreamt for a moment that her end was so near. I'm expecting a letter from Hinewai any day now to let me know of her baby's death. Len and Hinewai must feel their loss very keenly.

I must thank you for endeavouring to do your utmost to send me a reminder of Willow Glen. What became of Sandy, is he with your Uncle and Jess. I hear that the Pattersons are progressing favourably on their estate. Also, by all accounts the Browns at the homestead are very nice people and good neighbours.

As I have missed the last mail out for New Zealand before Christmas, I am sending some Christmas Cards as early as possible and will reach you sometime in January.

I don't expect that we will ever see the line again until the winter is over. But all the same I don't envy the brave boys who will be holding the line during the winter months.

Well, I must wish you and Granny, 'A Merry Xmas and a very Happy New Year'. Hoping you are both keeping well, trusting that 'ere this reaches you, I have got rid of my cold. I enclose lots of arohanui and may God be with you all until we meet again.

Please turn over for address.
Yours, friend Bill.

The letters that Wiremu sent back to his friend gave only a glimpse of the severe conditions and tragic losses that the Pioneers encountered on the wet, cold, muddy battlefields. It was astonishing that the soldiers could continue to maintain a cheerful exchange, given the atrocities they witnessed. The humour and good spirit of the Battalion members were among its most outstanding characteristics.

The Battalion had a few days' rest at the beginning of November, and amid the training and wet weather, they staged a sports event.

Changes at home

A Māori soldier enjoying a cigar gifted by Sir Joseph Ward, deputy leader of New Zealand's administration for the First World War, during a June 1918 visit at Bois de Warnimont, France.
Auckland War Memorial Museum Tamaki Paenga Hira, Photograph 689, album 419

'The mules in the New Zealand Pioneer Grand National Steeplechase provided the best race of the day. No spurs or whips allowed. C Company's *Pioneer Stew* led the field to the turn where he was challenged by D Company's *Pork & Beans* who, after a desperate finish, won by a head.'[5]

The break provided a chance to sharpen and hone skills on a number of fronts: 'The Bandmaster of 1st Canterbury kindly took charge of our Buglers and Drummers for a fortnight. They are now able to make a most joyful noise to cheer us on the march.'[6]

> France
> 6-11-17
>
> Dear Virgie
> I am in receipt of your letter dated Sept 3rd and have to thank you very much indeed for the lovely little book of poems you sent

along. It was very nice and kind of you for thinking of me. I think some of the verses in the book are very pretty and appropriate, don't you think so, especially the last one, Impatience. I only wish that it was really true. I have also to thank you for sending the parcel. At time of writing I have not yet received same but I am looking forward to getting it. Oh yes, I received the parcel of socks etc alright.

Yes, a trip to dear old New Zealand would be very nice. I am very sorry to hear of the death of my wee niece. Thank you very much for your sincere sympathy. Really, it's awful to think that such a dear wee kiddie should be taken away so soon and I have not had the pleasure of seeing her. Oh what rotten luck for me. I haven't heard from Hinewai or Len since their baby died. Dick Taiaroa wrote and told me first, then Joe Teihoka and yourself.

Please accept my deepest sympathy in your loss through the death of your cousin. I remember his name quite well. But never mind, he died nobly fighting for his King and Empire and loved ones at home.

Well Virgie, these heavy casualty lists over here must be heartbreaking to the people of New Zealand. Especially the last fight we took part in on the Ypres front was very heavy. The two Thian boys were slightly wounded. Jim Cannon escaped without a scratch. George Harper of Leeston, being a member of the band, never took part. I saw him soon after we came out. He is looking well. These are the only boys I have heard of since I left the line. I am also pleased to tell you that I have had the good luck to escape without being hit, so far.

I think the war will last a long time yet. Don't you think so? How about my prediction of five years warfare? You will find I won't be far out. The way things are going over here at present, it will take quite a long while to finish the war. Fancy the master being called up, eh. Well I hope that he won't be wanted, but I daresay before next spring we will want all available men over here to be able to give Fritz another pill to go on with, before peace is declared.

I know that you all must be worrying and anxiously waiting for the war to finish. As for us, the moving about and changes help break the monotony of warfare and the only time one really thinks of being in any danger and away from home is when he is under shell-fire.

The winter is right at hand and we have been given some heavy winter clothing, and it's pretty cold at night and early morning. I fancy you will be having a tip-top week for the Christchurch Show and races. Don't forget to let me know which horse won the NZ Cup, in fact both Cups, trotting and gallops. Did H.E. have any sheep or horses at the Show this year?

So, Emily's boy has been called up, eh. Tell Emily I'm sorry that I won't be able to come back and cheer her up while her boy is away doing his bit. However, she is not to worry. He'll never be killed. Tell her that I said so. Also tell her that she should be like me, have no one to worry over. That's why I am at the war. I think Emily will want to pull my hair if she could only get hold of me.

Well Virg. I must ring off as I have no more news to write. Hoping you are all well at home. I would like to ring you up tonight on your phone. But it's too far altogether.

'Cheer Oh' and Arohanui.
Remembrance to Granny and Emily, not forgetting your dear self.
Yours Sincerely
Friend Bill.

12

The onset of winter

In New Zealand, Phoebe had moved on and started her new life with William Anderson. Their first child, a son, was born in November 1917. They named him William. Phoebe had not given up hope of finding Marjorie Joyce, and she continued to search for a clue or snippet of information that might lead her to her daughter.

On 12 November, Wiremu's battalion was on the move again, heading to Dickesbusch, a two-day journey on foot and by train. The *War Diary* records, 'Owing to thick mist our guide lost his bearings but we finally reached camp at about 3.30 a.m. The Padre did yeoman service with the rear guard beating up the sick, lame and lazy, and none of the clever gentlemen who tried to tuck themselves away for a sleep by the roadside escaped his eagle eye.'[1]

Padre Henare Wainoho provided spiritual guidance and support to the men of the Pioneers. He reported back to the Bishop, 'Ka nui te pai me te kaha o nga tamariki Maori e noho atu nei. Ki taku titiro nui atu nga painga kua puta atu ki te iwi Maori i runga i nga ahuatanga maha o tenei whawhai. He nui nga akoranga pai kua homai ki ahau me aku tamariki, akoranga kaore nei e mau mai ki a matou ahakoa tae ki te 100 nga tau e noho ana ki Niu Tireni ra.'[2] [The Maori boys over here are fit and well. I believe a greater benefit will come to the Maori people as a result of their efforts in this war. My boys and I have gained a lot, lessons that we could never have learned from 100 years living in New Zealand.]

The Battalion resumed road maintenance and tramline formation work. The health of the Battalion was relatively good and their evacuations were well below the average of the Division.³ The seasons changed and the cold weather set in again, making conditions more difficult.

> In the Field
> 14-11-17
>
> Dear Virgie
> Just a few lines to let you know that I received the two paper parcels you sent along some time ago, for which I thank you very much. The busters were very interesting reading and you know it's just like being at home again to me, reading local news.
> Well, I am very proud of our wee district Sedgemere taking part in all the patriotic fund movements, raising no end of money to help us boys. Something to be proud of I can assure you.
> No doubt you would be wondering what became of me as I have not written for some considerable time. Matter of fact I made an attempt to write last month, but owing to our indefinite movements I had to cancel all correspondence until we had properly settled down. For nearly a week we were on the move from place to place so that I had no time whatever to write. However, now that we have temporarily settled down I am taking the first opportunity of writing.
> Well, we are up to our necks in mud just now. It has been raining nearly every day. Talk about being cold and miserable. It's something awful. Anyone can hardly realise the misery and hardships the boys have to contend with until witnessed personally. Why the mud sticks to our boots like glue. So you may guess that the snow and frost will be heartily welcomed to make the roads much better for traffic. We are expecting soon to go into winter quarters, finish war for two or three months to come, probably more and a nice quiet spot like we were at last year would be just the thing.
> Oh, really I must not forget to wish both Granny and yourself 'A Merry Christmas and Happy New Year' when it comes. I think by the time this reaches you Christmas will be close on hand.

Hoping that this coming one may be my last out here and the next one will be spent in dear old New Zealand but somehow I think my five year prediction will come true yet. What do you think eh?

I have only heard that the two Thian boys have been slightly wounded in our last fight. Also Charlie Halliday from Leeston. These are the only boys wounded that I have heard of.

I hear that Lieutenant Pohio is over in England at present waiting for the next draft to come over to join us. Yes, I had heard that he has run away with a lassie from Kaiapoi. I had one letter from Hinewai lately. They were all well. News is scarce just now.

Will now wish you both 'Au revoir' and arohanui, with best regards to Emily,

Yours sincere

Friend Bill

The men found distractions from the cold conditions including nights at the local *estaminets* for a few drinks and general socialising. They developed a reputation for getting rowdy and 'jeering at cavalrymen for being so far behind the line.'[4] Orders for the Pioneers to cease the practice of carrying blazing sticks of cordite around at night as torches were largely ignored.[5]

In the Field
12-12-17

Dear Virgie

Just a few lines to let you know that I'm still alive and well. Trusting that both Granny and yourself are enjoying the best of good health. At present we are having rather a fine winter considering the month is the middle of winter. Quite a contrast to Dec of 1916 where we had snow and frost galore. Of course it's quite early yet so snow and frost may fall at any time. At any rate I think every one of us would prefer to be without the snow and frost.

I daresay you have seen the papers some time ago to the effect that Lieutenant Pohio has been slightly wounded. He was no more than six to eight weeks with us when he got wounded but I am pleased to say it's not severe, only a light wound.

Today, I received a gift parcel from the Residents of Sedgemere per Mrs McLaughlin. Received in good condition containing cake, pudding, tin of salmon, tin of cocoa, 1 pr of socks, pocket handkerchief, packet of cigarette tobacco and papers and tin of cigarettes.

The parcel you sent has not arrived yet. As another New Zealand mail has just come in, quite likely it will turn up with this mail. Another parcel sent to me from Little River is not yet to hand and was sent about the time yours left, however I have no doubt that it will arrive in good time too. I bet you must have some lovely weather over there just now. I suppose everything is looking at its best, just the opposite of things over here and that's saying a great deal, for this is no catch over here. But I expect it won't last forever. If I could only last out long enough to see the finish I'll be quite satisfied. As one never knows how long he may last, it's best to carry on until one is knocked down.

I'm ashamed to say that I have been having another birthday celebration, but don't you think it rather early though? Well, I'll tell you how it happened. Four of us went out one evening to a small village where a cinema or picture show was being given. When we arrived we met several old pals and that was the end of the pictures. We went along to the nearest Estraminet — French Hotel and indulged pretty freely, until it was too late for pictures. Altogether we had rather an enjoyable evening out. We are to meet again on Christmas Eve when we hope to have a real old New Zealand spree, providing the cash is plentiful. There's one thing over here, liquor is very much cheaper so that we can have a tip-top time on half the money that we would have had in New Zealand.

Well now, I must really close as I have no more news for the present.

Kind regards and arohanui
Yours Sincerely
Friend Bill

❦ The Last *Maopo*

The Pioneers planned a Christmas feast of pork and potato hāngi and they collected pigs and beer for the occasion. A couple of days before Christmas, German planes flew over the Pioneers' camp just after dark, and dropped bombs. While the situation was very serious, with soldiers killed and wounded, 'the chief anxiety was as to the safety of the pigs which had been collected for Xmas but the excitement cooled down when it was found that neither these nor the beer had suffered.'[6]

The Commanding Officer's notes of Christmas Day record: 'The mid-day meal was a dreadful exhibition, but luckily Lord Rhondda [the British Food Controller] did not appear on the scene, and the Battalion relapsed into a more or less comatose state for the rest of the day, waking up somewhat towards evening to polish off the remainder of the feast.'[7]

> In the Field
> 15-12-17
>
> Dear Virgie
> I have the pleasure of acknowledging the receipt of a parcel sent by you, which duly arrived today containing the following, 1 tin of sugar, 2 tins of paste, 1 tin of cigarettes, sweets, chewing gum, milk chocolates, and a bottle of milk tablets which arrived in good condition. I wish you to extend to Granny and Emily many thanks also for their kindness to me. Really, I think you are true New Zealand lassies, to be proud of, and I will not forget your kindness to me.
> At present I am enjoying the best of good health. Trusting that you are all enjoying the same at home. We have not had any very bad weather to speak of, excepting for chilly freezes in the early morning and the snow has kept well away for the present.
> Now that Christmas is fast approaching I don't know what sort of time I'll have, at any rate, I intend to have a ding dong time, under the present conditions but nothing compared to the old times at Willow Glen.
> I have managed to get a rise as a Lance Corporal, at the time of writing am an Orderly Corporal.

A big New Zealand mail has arrived and the only mail for me was the parcel you sent. I have been carrying bags upon bags of letters but not one for me and you don't know how disappointed I have been not receiving anything. However, I have not given up all hopes yet. I do believe something may turn up for me before Xmas. I have been advised from my cousins at Little River to the effect that they have forwarded two parcels to me. So I won't be so badly off will I, eh?

How is Emily keeping? I am sure she must be worrying over her boy being called up. What a lucky thing for you that your boy has not been passed for 'Active Service'. I'm sure he should be very pleased with himself. I see in the New Zealand papers that we have no earthly chance of returning for leave. Stiff luck for us out here, eh.

Well, look here. Now that I have been out here now nearly three years I don't feel inclined to come back at all. I think I'll put all my money in the war loan and stay here, or rather over in 'Blighty'. I am expecting to get away on leave next month to Paris. It won't be my fault if I don't have a ripping time. I hear with twenty pounds a fellow can have a real good time, looking around sighting the scenery and visiting the most historical places of old.

Well Virg, really I must now conclude with best love to all,

Arohanui to Granny and Emily, not forgetting your dear self. Yours Sincerely, Bill.

L/Cpl W K Maopo
No 5 Platoon "B. Coy"
N.Z. Pioneers.

Twenty reinforcements arrived on Christmas Day and by the end of 1917 the Battalion comprised 928 men. The evacuation of sick soldiers was heavy during December and the weather turned cold, freezing the ground once again after snow fell on Christmas Day. In the New Year the construction of communication trenches, railway and road works continued at Ypres.

❦ The Last *Maopo*

A 'For Remembrance' card.
Author's collection

In the Field
22-1-18

Dear Virgie

Your letter of Nov 11th to hand a couple of days ago found me as usual enjoying the best of good health. Hoping these few lines will find you and Granny enjoying the same also. So you really think that the country is much preferable to town after all, eh? Well I guess town life ought not to be despised it will be a good change you know.

Thank you very much for your kind expressions of sympathy. Poor little missy, I was so sorry when I heard of her death. Also, I have to thank you very much for promising to send me a pair of mittens. They will come in very handy at present, as the cold weather is still prevailing over here. But speaking generally, we are having quite a mild winter, compared to last winter, being practically acclimatised, we don't feel the cold not so much now. Tell Granny that I sincerely hope to see her looking her best when I return. As for being alive, she will be very much alive when I get back.

Today I received such a friendly letter from young Emily and was very pleased to hear from her. I may say her letter came as a great surprise to me. But nevertheless I always welcome old friends' letters which help to take the war monotony away. I think by the time you receive this letter I will be away to Paris on 10 days leave. Hoping to return in time to go to 'Blighty' to catch the 'Royal Horse Show' held at Glasgow.

There is no news at all over here except of course war news, but you know more about that than I do, although I am right amongst it. I must not forget to tell you though that since I have been playing the game, that is to say not celebrating too many birthdays, I have been promoted to Lance Corporal. Probably some day I may have the good fortune to be recommended for a commission, who knows, eh. Don't you think I would make some officer, as we are always short of officers, I might happen to fluke it.

Well Virgie, I must now conclude with kind regards and arohanui to you both.

I remain yours sincerely
Friend Bill.

The work during January continued, with fewer casualties, but the freezing conditions saw many men succumb to illness, although the South Islanders were accustomed to cold winters and did not consider it particularly harsh.

In the Field
26-1-18

Dear Virginia

I have the greatest pleasure of acknowledging the receipt of the parcel you sent me containing pair of mittens and tin of coffee and milk mixture which arrived in excellent condition this evening, for which I thank you very much.

The mittens fit lovely and you should have seen the other boys admiring them, they fairly fell in love with them and wanted to know who sent them. Of course I told a lie that my best young lady sent them. One boy said he wished he had a nice young lady in New Zealand to send him a pair like mine. Therefore I will have to take care of mine otherwise someone will be making off with them.

The cloth wrapper you sent over outside of the tin came in handy for wrapping my small parcel which I'm sending to you of badge, shell casing ring and two French small handkerchiefs to replace those I had already sent, which have gone astray. I presume they have gone down to the bottom of the deep blue sea alright. Hoping you may have better luck to receive these as a small token of 'Friendships Sake'.

We are having a very mild winter, much like New Zealand spring weather. Also the days are beginning to lengthen out and we have only a few more days before we are in the spring season, which begins on the 18th of Feb. I have not been on leave yet for the second time, owing to shortage of cash. I have only cabled away to Wellington a few days ago for leave money so it won't be long now before going on leave, as I am due to go.

I have been offered Paris leave also, but will not go there, until I have been to 'Blighty' once more. I intend to visit the Glasgow Royal Horse Show this year if it can be possible to do so. Also visit the 'Lakes of Killarney' in Ireland. I believe they are just lovely, what do you think?

Emily wrote to say that her Dad expects that I will be bringing back a wife when I return to New Zealand but I don't think so, unless it's someone that has a lot of money and that's not everything is it, but mind you the Scotch lassies impressed me immensely. I was fairly interested with them. One couldn't help it. They are so nice and sociable, being not afraid to show one around sightseeing. Only you know, being of a shy sort, I practically managed to escape all entreaties, so will play the game like Joe Teihoka, wait until I return. That's if there are any unmarried young ladies about. Quite a number of boys over here have married English and Scotch lassies. I know several out of our Battalion that have been on leave and got married.

Well Virgie, I have not much news to say this time. Hoping you

are both well as I am at present. Again, thanking you very much
for parcel, I conclude with best regards and arohanui and love
to Emily.

Yours Sincerely, Friend Bill

In February the Pioneer Battalion was subject to further losses and 73 men were admitted to hospital for illness.[8] Work continued as they performed trench and wire activity. Wiremu's letters remained cheerful, although small references to the lasting effects of the war had begun to creep in. Emily Cant's young man, Cecil Hastings, also joined the war effort. Dave Fincham, Virgie's cousin, was called up. Dave's brother, Bruce, had also been raised by Granny at Willow Glen and was part of the Willow Glen 'gang', so they all knew of his brother Dave.

In the Field
4.2.18

Dear Virgie
Thank you very much for the Auckland Weekly News, Xmas number, which I received a few days ago. I think it was the best one I have seen for many a long time and the different scenery and pictures are simply lovely. I have all the pictures hung up in our dugout, which looks quite flash.
You know I expected to be away on leave before this month but owing to my remittance from New Zealand not having arrived I am unable to go until I hear from our Staff Paymaster to the effect that the money has arrived. However, I daresay when it does arrive the weather too will be just lovely and everything over there looking their best. Ladies included, of course.
I hope both Granny and yourself are enjoying the best of health as I am at present. Things are very quiet just now. The weather very cold and chilly in the early morning and evening but during the middle of the day it's just nice, like our own spring weather in the middle of October.
I received a Press last week but I do not know who the kind

sender is, also a lot of papers, Star Evening News and The Sun, and all Christchurch papers. As no names were on the papers to enlighten me who the senders were, I was unable to know but all the same I am very thankful to them. I see by the papers a great fire took place in Christchurch some time ago, burning several buildings amounting to thousands of pounds. What a big loss. Have they found out the cause of the fire? Perhaps some spies may have done so, eh.

I have also seen photos of several boys from the Ellesmere district that have been killed and wounded over here. No doubt this war is thinning out far too many of our boys, don't you think, and those who have been wounded and returned will be wrecks for all time. What a shame, it's awful when one thinks of it. I have seen just too much over here and I don't think that I will be too willing to volunteer in the next war, that is of course, if I get back after this one. I'm looking well ahead, ain't I now. I suppose nothing like it.

So, Charlie Cooper is the only Cooper representative coming out to meet the enemy eh, probably Robbie too. However, I am pleased and I hope to meet him over here. I suppose if he is with the Mounteds, Palestine will be his destination, likewise Dave Fincham. Fancy young Dave coming out. He can't be very old, can he? Why, it doesn't seem so long ago when he was wearing short trousers. How did Granny take it, she will be awfully cut up, won't she?

As for Cecil Hastings, he will be here soon too. What about the Skillings and McCormicks and Howsons, what are they doing I wonder?

Oh, I say Virgie, I met an old friend of yours up the line a week ago. Looking well and has been promoted to Lance Corporal. He has been over here just over eight months so he is doing alright, better known as Bob Manson, late of Sedgemere, Davie Manson is here also but never met him last week. Bob tells me that Davie is alright. I am very pleased to know that they are still going strong for they have been doing some very dangerous work lately, and subject to face all kinds of shells that the Huns

are using against us. He and I had a good old yarn, of course
Taumutu and Sedgemere were brought in as our main talk,
not forgetting those good old dances we used to have in the
Woolshed, in the days of long ago when we were all young.

Bob tells me that like myself, he is fed up with everything out
here. I don't know how he will take things when he is over here
as long as me.

Well Virgie, I don't mind telling you I am getting a lot of grey
hairs on the head and looking very old. Of course you know I
am getting on in years. The old birthday next month. Hope to
be on leave then, whato then eh?

Yes, tell Granny I must see her before she goes West. I hope that she
may be spared for years and years yet. However, she must not talk
of dying yet. Why, tell her that she will be listening to me cackling
again before the next Christchurch Show comes round again.

Well Virg. I have no more news for you for the present. Really
there is no news at all but I must say something sometimes just
for old time's sake.

With regards to you and Granny and also Emily.
Cheerio and Arohanui
Yours Sincerely,
Friend Bill.

Rugby games were the highlight of recreational activities. The Pioneers fielded a Māori team to play against their Pākehā comrades, defeating them 50–3. Members of the Pioneers also played in the New Zealand Division team. When the Division team played against the French at Parc de Prince in Paris in 1918, a Māori soldier walked on to the field to lead the team in a haka prior to the game starting; New Zealand won the match.[9]

The Māori Pioneers had taken haka to the world with their performance of the dance during battles at Gallipoli, on occasions of visits by dignitaries during Division inspections and prior to rugby games. Their example has now endured as an international tradition for a hundred years.

❦ The Last *Maopo*

Māori soldiers perform a haka of welcome for government ministers led by Prime Minister Massey at Bois de Warnimont, France on 30 June 1918.
Auckland War Memorial Museum Tamaki Paenga Hira, Photograph 680, album 419

Letters from home were a lifeline for the soldiers and the wait for letters and packages would seem an age, especially as many were lost or delayed in transit.

> In the Field
> 28-2-18
>
> Dear Virgie
> I have received today your letter, dated Dec 16th, and I must thank you very much indeed for your thoughtfulness, sending me snapshots of yourself, Granny, our old pet Bluey, and the new 'Bungalow'. Some house I guess. I think the snap young Emily took of yourself is rather nice, and I don't mind saying that I couldn't help admiring your snaps every chance I could possibly get. I used to get out your snaps and have a look, reminding me of those good old days and times spent at Willow Glen. You can hardly imagine the pleasure and gladness the snaps stirred within me when gazing on them, poor old Granny looks very

old, doesn't she. I couldn't but help laughing to myself, when looking at her snap, about those old times when she used to roar at me for cackling at the table, comes back to memory.

Well Virg, I am unable to give account why my letters are not arriving more regular than at present, as I write every fortnight as regular as clockwork. Undoubtedly some have gone down, also the badge and shell casing ring, but I have again sent another quite recently and I sincerely hope that you will have more fortune to receive these. Your letters too have not been coming over so regular as before. I have heard that one New Zealand mail has been lost coming over here from New Zealand and I have not received letters from Hinewai or Len either for about 8 or 9 months.

When I wrote to you last month I expected to be proceeding to England on furlough, but owing to my remittance from New Zealand not having yet arrived, I couldn't go. I am expecting to hear from our Staff Paymaster at any time now, that the money has arrived and I intend to have a real good time. I will be on leave 'ere my birthday falls, so you can bet your life that yours truly will have some time, bon temps as the French people say, meaning good time, I am not very fluent with the French language but can make myself understood when asking for eatables and cigarettes and such like goods, however it's rather nice to be able to speak the language fairly well.

I am keeping fairly well at present and always looking forward to the day when I shall be able to bid this country farewell, which I sincerely hope to be very soon. Though I have no cause to grumble as I have had a fair spin since I left New Zealand, haven't I now. Going on for the third year next September 18th and I have not been wounded so far, but I don't mind telling you that I have been pretty close to being hit. Yes, Daddy has at last been hit, but I am pleased to say that he was only slightly hit and I hear that he is now almost himself again and was out of hospital on leave over in Blighty when last seen by one of our boys who recently returned from leave.

I must again thank you for the Xmas parcel which I received in the best of condition, also the pair of mittens which also arrived just when I was badly in need of a pair, but now the weather is simply lovely, so I have put them away for next winter, if we have the misfortune to be still over here. I must thank you also for the promise of the Balaclava you are making for me. No doubt I have a great deal to thank you for, for your kindness to me has been exceedingly great and I can hardly thank you enough, but however I do hope that I may be spared some day to return to New Zealand and thank you for all that I have received personally. I think I can safely say that you are just like a big sister to me, and I wish that I really had one, so kind to me as you have been, not only sending comforts and luxury but also writing so often to help cheer me up, as sometimes I get very down on my luck when I never hear from Hinewai or Len. I wrote to them last month telling them that if I don't hear from them soon I shall not write any more. You wouldn't very well blame me eh.

Will you please observe my present address. Your last letter went astray to my old address and I didn't get the letter for 3 or 4 days after its arrival at our field post office. L/cpl W.K. Maopo, No 8 Platoon, B Coy, NZ Maori (Pioneer) Batte. C/o GPO Wellington, my number as usual.

I must not forget to tell you that our Pioneer badges have been done away with. Our badges at present are the first badges we got when we first left New Zealand, that is the Maori badges, of which I sent you the embroidery fancy work from Egypt, you remember, and I think they are more appropriate than the Pioneer Badge.

I am sending you at first opportunity a book called NZ at the Front. It's all about our boys over here, humorous sketches, stories and poetry written by fellows serving over here, with us. There is also written in this book the story of the time our Battalion was sent up to help the French Army last year just after the capture of the Messines Ridge by our boys and other troops who worked famously together on that great memorable day, when we helped to add another great victory to our long list of victories which you have already read of in the papers.

> *Hoping both Granny and yourself are enjoying the best of good health.*
>
> *Kia ora and arohanui and best love to Emily*
> *From yours sincerely friend Bill.*

The changeable weather of March resulted in an increased number of cases of illness. Lieutenant Pohio fell ill with malaria and was sent to hospital.[10] The men prepared to move on from Flanders and their Commanding Officer noted: 'the amount of extra blankets and gear our young gentlemen had collected 'round themselves during our nearly three month stay in Ypres was appalling. We got it all away and were ready waiting first thing on the morning of the 22nd. At 7 p.m. we got orders and by 9.15 p.m. the Battalion was clear of Ypres and on the road to camp near Ouerdom. Fritz gave us a few parting shots as we passed shrapnel corner but otherwise we were not disturbed.'[11]

Taking a break from work: Māori pioneers working in the forward trenches near Gommecourt, 25 July 1918.
Auckland War Memorial Museum Tamaki Paenga Hira, Photo H 831, Album 419

13

Military hospital

The winter cold and the rough living conditions took a toll on the soldiers and led to many forms of illness. Almost three years after leaving home, and having survived the harshest of battle conditions, Wiremu succumbed to pneumonia and pleurisy. On 31 March 1918 he was taken by field ambulance to the military hospital. The local Taumutu newspaper kept the community appraised of Wiremu's condition, reporting in April that he was dangerously ill and then in May that his condition was improving. After being initially treated in France, Wiremu was sent to England to recover in the New Zealand General Hospital.

New Zealand War Contingent Association
Te Arohanui Club
No. 2 New Zealand General Hospital
Oatlands Park, Weybridge

3.5.18

Dear Virgie
Quite a considerable time now has lapsed since I last wrote and as you are now well aware of the fact that things have livened up again on this side of the globe, we have been having rather a busy time moving about like a real wild west show, so I had really no time whatever to write to you all until I had settled down, but it was not to be.
On arrival at our destination where all the fun was, I only had

four days amongst the real dinkum sport when I was overtaken with Pleuro-pneumonia and was sent away from the boys to a British Hospital where I was laid up for three weeks and four days, then was sent across to 'Blighty' where I am at present at the above Hospital and progressing favourably. But the third day I was in Hospital in France, I took a very bad turn and nearly went west, temperature was over 104° and how on earth I recovered is a mystery to the Doctors, Sisters and also to myself, for I knew absolutely nothing for quite an hour or more, after I did return to consciousness I was so weak that I could hardly speak. But by jove I will never forget the Sisters, they saved me and they couldn't do enough for me when I was marked out for Blighty. One Sister told me that she had a good mind not to let me go, for she looked upon me as part of the wood furniture, all Scotch Sisters they were. At present if you were to see me, you would hardly recognise me, nothing but skin and bone. Six weeks before I took ill I don't think I ever felt better in all my life, looking really well. It was simply a cold I contracted whilst travelling to our new destination and it gradually took a hold on me. It was sleeping out anywhere in the cold damp air which brought it on so quickly. However, I am very pleased to say that I am returning to New Zealand shortly as soon as I am strong enough. My papers have been sent away two days ago to be approved of at Medical Headquarters. So by the time this reaches you, yours truly will be well on his way back to dear old New Zealand, never to roam any more.

Well Virgie, I have not received any letters from you for some time. A New Zealand mail has just arrived so I will be getting some mail, but I suppose they will all be sent across to France first. How are you and Granny keeping, quite well I hope? I will write again soon. In all probability I will be sailing in about a month's time, and I am looking forward to getting sick leave before I leave old Blighty and Scotland. As I have no more news to tell you I will now conclude with kind remembrance to you both and Emily.

Kia ora and Arohanui
Yours Sincerely, Bill

❦ The Last *Maopo*

Wiremu's health was still fragile. The pneumonia had left him weak and had damaged his lungs. He was classified as unfit to return to the field and was to be sent home to New Zealand on extended sick leave. He would finally have the chance to see friends and family and visit his home. A delay in transport meant that Wiremu had time to see more of the sights of England and Scotland before he returned to New Zealand.

> New Zealand War Contingent Association
> Te Arohanui Club
> No.2 New Zealand General Hospital
> Oatlands Park, Weybridge
>
> 29.6.18
>
> Dear Virgie
> Today your kind and welcome letter dated Jan 25th arrived after following me around from the time I left the Battalion until I arrived here. Of course I wrote away to our Staff Post Master notifying him of my whereabouts, but probably they overlooked matters and sent my mail across to France. Please forgive lead-pencil writing as I have already tried six pens and none of them were any good.
> Well Virgie, I am pleased to hear that both Granny and yourself are keeping well. At present I am keeping fairly well. I have got over my sickness but have had a slight attack of the influenza. I must thank both Emily and yourself for the snap of Emily you sent me, really, well, you know not bad for an amateur photographer, is it?
> Well, I wrote and told you some time ago that I am returning to New Zealand on sick furlough, you know I was to sail last month but I was kept back until a hospital ship was available. Just as well too, because I applied for sick furlough over here and got three weeks leave. I went up to Aberdeen, Scotland, to Glasgow, Edinburgh and Carlisle. You have heard Johnny Mossop speak of Carlisle before haven't you? Well, I enjoyed my leave immensely. While at Carlisle I visited munitions works,

lakes and forest, Carlisle Castle and army barracks. Whilst at Glasgow I visited Glasgow Herald printing works, Shipbuilding yards, torpedo boat building yards, all the historic shell making works employing 5,000 girls, and a trip on the Clyde River. After this I went on to Edinburgh and visited all the places of interest there. I went out to see the Forth bridge and went on board the warship New Zealand while she was in dock. Last but not least Watson's whiskey distillery works, all the sea resorts around Edinburgh then on to Aberdeen. Owing to the wet weather while I was at Aberdeen I was unable to go out much. So I didn't stop there long. I returned to Carlisle for a few days before I came down to London.

Of course I saw all the sites around London last year so I took things very quietly until my time was up to report back to Hospital. Together I enjoyed my trip very much. I shall tell you all about it again when I come back. I like being up in Scotland much better than England. You know it cost me £35 for the three weeks I was away, then I had £5 to spare when I finished up, not bad for me, eh.

When I left the Battalion in France we were in the line at the time, just when the German offensive began in March. Well, I left all my gear behind, letters I got from you and Xmas cards I received from you all. They were all stolen. I wrote back for them and got word that they were all taken away. Look, I nearly cried. Only fancy keeping all those cards all this long time and just when I wanted them badly I had the misfortune to lose them. But the snaps you sent me I have with me. I carried them right through the piece and they are the only things that I have to bring back.

Well now, I must really ring off as I have no more to say. Please don't reply. I shall be nearly home when you get this.

So Cheerio and Kia Ora.
Until we meet again.
Yours sincerely, friend Bill.

14

Wiremu returns home

After three years serving in the war and surviving the battlefields of Flanders, Messines and Passchendaele, Wiremu was sent home on sick leave to recover from his serious bout of pneumonia. He arrived by boat into Lyttelton Harbour on 24 September 1918. Hinewai's husband, Len Cant, met him at the port in Lyttleton. On the way home Len told Wiremu that Virgie had married John Mossop and moved to the North Island. Johnny had worked at Willow Glen as a cowman. While disappointed not to be able to catch up with Virgie, Wiremu's prediction that he would see Granny before the next Christchurch show was to be proved correct. He was delighted when Len took him by tram to visit Granny at her new home in Christchurch before heading home to Taumutu.

A week or so after his return, a community gathering was held to welcome Wiremu and other soldiers home. On 4 October 1918, at 8 p.m., ladies were invited to bring a plate of refreshments and gents two shillings, for the occasion. Reverend Butler was the principal speaker for the evening and his comments were reported in the *Ellesmere Guardian*:

> It was not an easy matter to thank men who had been through what the guests had faced in order to preserve the liberty of mankind. They had been willing to sacrifice life itself for the great cause. It

was a good thing for people to realise what they had been protected from. When one read of the atrocities committed upon our soldiers by the enemy it almost made us ashamed of the human race. We remembered, however, that we were Britishers and that our men had not stained their hands as the enemy soldiers had done.

'We were all proud to think that the people of Southbridge were doing so much to support and encourage the boys at the front,' said L. Corpl Maopo. The parcels they had sent had helped a great deal to brighten the lives of the soldiers. When he was being taken to the hospital after being wounded [sic], the first shirt given to him had Southbridge stamped upon it. The YMCA was a great organisation. It had supplied him with many a good hot drink and his requests for cigarettes had never been refused.

The Sedgemere community also held a special event advertised as the 'Welcome Home Social to Lance Corporal Maopo'. The social was also reported in the *Ellesmere Guardian*:

A splendid gathering assembled at the Sedgemere Hall on Friday night to extend a welcome home to Lance Corporal W.K. Maopo, a well known Taumutu man, who arrived back from the front a fortnight ago, after three years' service. The attendance at the function of people from the surrounding districts was alone sufficient to apprise anyone of the fact that the soldier was a popular young fellow. The proceedings were of a hearty character throughout. Dancing was kept up with great spirit until past two on Saturday morning, Mesdames Lambie and Campbell presiding on the piano in turn, while assistance was also given by other musicians. Messrs J. Martin and V.J. Leahy shared the duties of MC. Songs were sung by Messrs W. Marsh and J. Teihoka.

Lance Corporal Maopo was the recipient of a very fine silver wristlet watch from his friends. Mr J.T. Parkin, who presided, made the presentation and in the course of a short speech said that the residents esteemed it a special pleasure to be able to welcome the guest back into their midst. Lance Corporal Maopo had enlisted with the 2nd Maori Battalion and was away from the district before the people were really aware he was going, and in consequence there had been no send-off social to him. They were determined, however, that he should receive a very hearty welcome home. The Maoris at Taumutu had put up a fine record in the matter of military service. At the outbreak of war there were only some half-dozen First Division men at Taumutu, and five of them went away with the 2nd Maori Battalion. The Maoris were a race to be proud of. They knew what German rule meant and were determined to have none of it. That determination had been backed up by the offer of their lives in the cause of freedom.

On the stage with the guest were Privates W. Beamsley and D. McMillian, both of whom returned along with Lance-Corporal Maopo. They were accorded a hearty welcome by the chairman, whose words were warmly approved by all in the hall. Two other soldiers who are about to leave for the front, Corporal Stretz and Trooper Boyd, were also present and to them the chairman conveyed the best wishes of the people of Sedgemere for an early and safe return.

Mr R.M. Taiaroa said that Lance Corporal Maopo had left at his country's call and had served his King for a period of three years. Any man who answered his country's call was entitled to all honour the people could bestow upon him, for was he not offering to lay down his life if need be for their sake? The guest had served on Gallipoli and in France. He was sure that all present lamented the fact that three of the young fellows who had gone away with Lance Corporal Maopo would never return to their native land. Cheerfully they had given their all that the great blessing of freedom which was so dear to the heart of both Maori and Pakeha alike should be handed down to future generations. Like many others who had returned, Lance Corporal Maopo had found a vacant chair at the domestic fireside.

They had every reason to rejoice over the war news of the last week or two. At last the Allies were able to force the enemy back, in spite of all his defences, and they were not going to stop until complete victory was achieved and the enemy was made to pay for the wrongs he had committed.

> *Lance Corporal Maopo made a suitable reply, in the course of which he gave an interesting account of his experiences.*
>
> *Private Beamsley, who replied of behalf of Private McMillan and himself, spoke very highly of the work done by the Maoris at the front. The NZ Pioneers had proved themselves second to none at entrenching work and in the erection of wire entanglements. They were also splendid soldiers. When the first batch of American soldiers reached France and wanted to know how the men went 'over the top', thirty Maori soldiers were selected to give them the object lesson. That was a good indication of what the authorities thought of the Maoris. Corporal Stretz also made a short reply, after which supper was served.*

Wiremu was pleased to be home and was working on his recovery. He was well aware that this might only be a short respite from the war and he could soon be sent back. Much had changed at home in the few years that he had been away. His father had died, Phoebe and the Schnelles were gone, Willow Glen had been sold and the Finchams had moved away. His good friend Virgie Fincham had married Johnny Mossop and the pair had moved to a dairy farm in Tokoroa, in the North Island. Wiremu continued to correspond with Virgie and keep her apprised of news from Taumutu.

> *Mrs John Mossop*
> *Tokoroa*
> *Putaruru*
> *Waikato, NZ*
>
> *Taumutu*
> *14-10-18*
>
> *Dear Mrs Mossop*
> *Please accept my heartiest congratulations and I sincerely hope that you may be very happy indeed and have a long married life before you. I hope that both John and yourself are enjoying the best of good health. Since I have been home I have been enjoying the best of health.*

I am trying to discharge but I am not certain whether I shall get a discharge as I only returned on sick furlough. Now that I am getting well again I suppose I shall be going back to the front once more.

I find things pretty quiet just now. Went to see Grandma and Mrs Duffell twice, met Emily once in town, and I only hope I shall see you before I go back. I won't be going back before Xmas.

I got a big turnout at the Sedgemere Hall. I was presented with a wristlet-illuminated watch, which cost eight pounds eight and a little beauty it is too. I am going in to town to see Emily next week. Well news is scarce.

So Goodbye and Cheerio.
Yours, old friend Bill.

PS What do you think. Poor Mrs Howson died last Friday morning from heart trouble. Oh how sad.

Taumutu
6/11/18

Dear Virgie

Many thanks for your kindness in sending me a piece of your wedding cake, which arrived yesterday in excellent condition and I can hardly express my feelings of thanks again. Please extend to John my compliments of gratitude, hoping that both John and yourself shall live long and happily together. Also give my best wishes to Burkitt. Really I never expected to receive anything, of course I was only joking when I wrote from France asking you not to forget old Bill when your time came and sure enough you kept your word. Well Virgie, I enjoyed your cake, lovely, and if I may have the luck also to get my discharge I shall settle down too. Then I shall send you a piece of mine.

Yes, Granny and Emily were pleased to see me and I only wished that you were at Granny's the day I arrived at Christchurch. After dinner Len and I went out to see Granny. Jove, you would have laughed when Len and I got to the house. Granny and Algy were out planting cabbages and potatoes and both were busily engaged at work when all at once I called her and began to laugh. Oh, poor old soul, she was pleased. She asked us in and don't forget, the wine decanter got well emptied. However, she told me that she only wished you had been here to see me back before you went up North. You know, I was thunderstruck when Len told me on our way out to Granny's that you had taken flight from Christchurch and got married.

I think the house is awfully beautiful, both flower and kitchen gardens are looking lovely. I was greatly taken with your wedding group. I only wished that you had one to spare. I would have liked one very much. I don't know whether I will be returning to France again or not but I am still under medical treatment at present. I am looking well and fit too but I don't want to go back to the war again.

I have got my photo taken in town the other day and if any good, worth giving away, I will send one up for you, if you will accept it.

Len and Hinewai wished to be remembered to both John and yourself.

I met Mr and Mrs H.E. Fincham and Sandy at the Leeston Show. They were pleased to see me back once more. The show was absolutely rotten, very quiet indeed, but I enjoyed myself talking to my old friends. Hinewai is sick in bed with the influenza. In fact everybody around here is sick with the influenza.

Well Virgie, again I thank you very much. I will write again after the show and races are over. Trusting you are all well.

Kia ora and Goodbye
Yours Sincerely
Friend
W.K. Maopo

❦ The Last *Maopo*

Wiremu Maopo. Given to the author's mother by Malcolm Ward. The photo had belonged to Malcolm's late mother; Wiremu boarded with her family for a time prior to his death.
Author's collection

Wiremu's health did not recover sufficiently for him to return to fight in the war. His prediction of a five-year war was not far wrong. The war ended in November 1918, almost four and a half years after it began. It was some months before the Battalion returned home.

Granny was not spared the tragedy of war. Her grandson, Dave Fincham, died merely four days before Armistice was declared. He had been writing home and making good-humoured jibes at his grandmother's short stature, asking, 'How is Granny, is she still growing?'

Wiremu was discharged from the Army on 22 November 1918 after three years and five months (147 days) of service. He had survived the war and was presented with the British War Medal and the Victory Medal. With his parents gone and Hinewai now his only surviving sibling, Wiremu was faced with restarting his life at Taumutu. The effects of the war remained with him and his health continued to suffer. He spent his time between the military hospital in Cashmere and at home in Taumutu.

Taumutu
23/6/19

Mrs John Mossop
Waikato

Dear Virgie

Will you please forgive me for not answering your long overdue letter. I was away on sick furlough and then I have been in town for further medical treatment, as the cold and frosty weather which have been prevailing have been against my health, however better late than never. I trust that both John and yourself are enjoying the best of health. I am not in the best of health at present, also Len has been ill with Rheumatic fever and has been away up to Hanmer Springs for nearly 2 months now. Hinewai is away to see him just now, she is well.

I am batching all alone and doing fine. Quite a sensation was astir on the 7th of this month (June) at the Sedgemere Hall, the event was the unveiling of our Roll of Honour Board and such a lovely piece of work. Mr Rodgers the builder of Leeston made the Board of varnished Oak wood and each soldier's name was in large gold lettering, which looks lovely. The Hall was simply crowded and even outside of the Hall there were a lot of people who were unable to find room inside.

There was a military parade of Returned men, Territorials and Cadets. Colonel Chaffey, who unveiled the Board, also inspected the parade. The Mayor of Christchurch (Dr Thacker) was also present. He, after the unveiling, presented Gold medals to the following boys and next of kin. Medals for George and Huri Taiaroa, who were absent (Mrs Taiaroa), Bert McGill (Mr McGill), Willie Edwards also absent, to his father. As Fred Stretz's medal was not finished it was not presented. Joe Teihoka and I were the only two who were present to receive ours personally, in between speeches.

Songs were given and after partaking of afternoon tea we all went away quite pleased with the afternoon, but more pleased with the

> Sedgemere–Taumutu Honour Board. The medals are beauties of nine carat gold, costing over 1 guinea each.
>
> Last Thursday evening a Bachelors Ball was held in the Sedgemere Hall in aid of a clubroom for Returned Soldiers in the Southbridge district. The takings were £7-6. The Hall was fairly well packed. Another piece of news I am sure may interest you is John Lochhead's old farm next to Leahy's has changed hands again. The purchaser being Alex McLaughlin (Taumutu) at £26 an acre.
>
> How are things doing up your way. Quite alright I hope. Hinewai had a letter from young Emily last week and she told her she had been up to see John and you. Well Virgie, no more news for the present.
>
> With best wishes to you both.
> Yours sincere, Friend Bill.

Wiremu's health was variable, but he recovered sufficiently to be able to resume a place in the Lakeside and Sedgemere football team, playing an occasional match against the Southbridge Football Club.

In October 1921 the Sedgemere community unveiled their roll of honour. Reverend Walker took the occasion to reflect on the toll that the war had taken:

> It had been calculated that seven million men had died of wounds or disease during the war and that another twenty million had been injured. The war debt had run into thirty thousand million sterling and the loss of property on the Western front alone was estimated at three hundred millions. Sixteen thousand men from our own Dominion had given their lives and 40,000 others had returned more or less injured. We must never forget the war but seek to lay to heart the lessons it has taught us. Tragic though the struggle had been, there were some things that tended to make our heart glad. There was cause to rejoice that in the time of trial the nation fainted not.

Earl Haig had said that the margin by which the German onrush in 1914 was stemmed was so narrow that the word miraculous was not too strong a term to use in describing the recovery and victory of the Allies.

Over 2200 Māori had volunteered to serve in the First World War. In an Anzac Day address in 1926, Sir Maui Pomare gave expression to the sentiment of the Māori soldiers in the service of their country: 'Make this beloved country of ours, the country for which we gave our lives, a better and a happier land for the children, for all who are to come after us.'[1]

15

Life after war

The last ten years of Wiremu's life were spent back at Taumutu. Sadly, his only remaining sibling, his sister Hinewai, died in March 1926, aged 35. She had been to see the Otago Exhibition in Dunedin and died at Karitane Hospital. Being the last survivors of the Maopo whānau, Hinewai and Wiremu were close. Wiremu was 40 and now the sole survivor of the once large Maopo family.

'Mop' Manning (right) and Remu Rehu.
Photograph supplied by Richard Manning

Unmarried and with no one to succeed him, Wiremu spoke with his mother's whānau, who lived at the other end of the lake at Wairewa, about finding a successor for the Maopo family lands. They agreed that Moloney Te Morokiekie Manning would be a whāngai for Wiremu. He became known by the Maopo nickname 'Mop'.

In May 1927 Wiremu made out his will, leaving the Maopo whānau land interests to his 'nephew', Te Morokiekie Manning.[1]

In the three years after Hinewai died, Wiremu moved around the district and boarded with local friends and relatives.[2] He sold or gifted some of the whānau lands and left the remainder for Mop to inherit.

Wiremu passed away on 12 July 1929, aged 43. He died from inflammation of the lungs and heart, a result of the conditions that he had contracted during the war. His mother's relatives buried him on a hill in Little River Māori Cemetery, at Wairewa. The Taumutu community and Wiremu's extended whānau farewelled the last member of the once-large Maopo whānau.

Wiremu's whāngai son Mop was in the North Island undertaking studies when Wiremu died. He was shocked to hear of the death on his return home and disappointed that Wiremu had not been buried with the rest of his family in the Hone Wetere urupā.

Wiremu's final resting place has a beautiful view of the valleys, lake and sea, overlooking the lands and waterways that were home to his people. His death marked the end of an era of Maopo whānau residing in this rohe (territory).

16

Finding Marjorie Joyce

For 12 years Phoebe continued to search for the daughter to whom Wiremu was father. Her efforts paid off and she finally located her. Phoebe made contact with the adopting family and obtained their consent to send letters and gifts to Marjorie Joyce.

It was a joyful day when she was reunited with her daughter. Phoebe's husband came with her and she presented Marjorie Joyce with a beautiful jewellery set and told her the story of her adoption. Phoebe wanted her daughter to know that she had not been willingly given away. She continued to visit her each year.

The news that she was adopted came as a shock to Marjorie Joyce, and she distanced herself from the family that had raised her, becoming aloof for a considerable period of time. Throughout the rest of her life she maintained contact with her birth mother, and regularly sent Phoebe flowers on Mother's Day. In later life Marjorie Joyce resumed a close relationship with her adopted family.

Marjorie Joyce left home and married Victor Davis. They eventually settled in Otorohanga, a short distance from where Fred and Emma Schnelle were living at Oparure. Each year Phoebe and her husband spent Easter holidays with Marjorie Joyce and Victor. Marjorie Joyce became close to Phoebe's second daughter, her half-sister Bonny (Madeleine Olive Bonsy). Bonny lived with Marjorie Joyce and Victor

Marjorie Joyce and Phoebe.
Photograph supplied by Maxine Allan

Marjorie Joyce with the Harman family. Rear left to right: Eunice, Marjorie Joyce, Clemens, Vera. Front: Elizabeth May.
Photograph supplied by Patricia Adams

for a period, working in the Otorohanga cinema, and Marjorie Joyce named her youngest daughter Madeline Fiona after her.

Phoebe married twice after her relationship with Wiremu (Bill), and both of her husbands were also named Bill. She had a son named Bill and daughter Bonny to her husband Bill Anderson. She then married Bill England and had a daughter named Betty. Phoebe told her daughters that she had children to three men, all called Bill, but that the first Bill was her true love.

Phoebe had no knowledge that Wiremu had survived the war. She also did not know of the letters that Wiremu had sent her, until she was told about them much later in her life. By this time the letters had been destroyed. She died believing what her parents had told her, that Wiremu had died in the war, never learning that this was a lie and that Wiremu had survived.

Wiremu was living at Taumutu at the time Phoebe found Marjorie Joyce. Neither he nor Phoebe had the right information to be able to reconnect. Wiremu died shortly after Phoebe had found Marjorie Joyce.

Marjorie Joyce had four children, a son Brian and three daughters, Maxine, Marilyn and Madeline (Fiona). As far as they could tell, she never knew the story of her father.

The whakapapa ledger closed on the Maopo whānau in 1929 with the death of Wiremu, the last Maopo. Had Wiremu known of Phoebe's plight, and that only a few hours' travel separated him from Phoebe and his daughter, the ending of his story might have been different. It would be 80 years before the Maopo whakapapa ledger would be reopened to recognise Wiremu's descendants.

17

Whakapapa Ngāi Tahu

After I (the author) received the letter from Taumutu Rūnanga making the connection to Wiremu Maopo, a number of experiences followed.

Millie Schnelle wrote to me. Now in her eighties, Millie was a child when her Aunty Phoebe lived with her at Taumutu. My mother visited Millie in hospital, and Millie told us all she could remember about Wiremu and Phoebe's romance. Sadly, Millie died a few days after my mother's visit.

An important final step in making the reconnection was to inform the tribal records of our existence, and to see if Wiremu's descendants would be recognised as Ngāi Tahu descendants. Richard Manning introduced us to Terry Ryan of Whakapapa Ngāi Tahu, who very graciously acknowledged our history.

Coincidentally, Terry had a conversation with Garth Cant, a lecturer at the University of Canterbury. Garth's father, Len Cant, had been married to Wiremu's sister, Hinewai.

Garth informed Terry that he had very recently been given a collection of letters from three soldiers of the Taumutu area who had fought in the First World War, including Wiremu Maopo. The soldiers had written to the Fincham family of Willow Glen; Virgie Fincham had responded on behalf of the family and a regular exchange of correspondence had developed between Virgie and the soldiers. The other two soldiers were Henry Pohio and Fred Stretz. Virgie had kept the letters from the soldiers at her home in Tokoroa. When she died, Joan Overhill, her niece, took care of the letters. Joan was then in her eighties and she passed the letters to Garth as she knew he was involved with the Historical Society and that he would be a responsible custodian. The letters had, in effect, returned to Taumutu after a century of safe keeping.

Terry told Garth of our recent contact with the Ngāi Tahu whakapapa unit in relation to Wiremu Maopo. Through Terry's introduction to Garth and the letters, the doors opened on our family history and our great-grandfather spoke to us in his own words. To know him through second- and third-hand references was fascinating, but to hear him speaking was an incredible gift.

A special occasion that marked the reconnection was an invitation facilitated by Garth Cant to attend the 125th Anniversary Service of the Hone Wetere Church at Taumutu. This is the marae church that Atarea Te Maiharanui Maopo had helped H.K. Taiaroa build, and in which he had served as a lay preacher. The invitation was to read a passage during the service alongside Richard Taiaroa, as the descendants and representatives of our ancestors. This was not only a great privilege, but it was also a symbolic reconnection for our whānau.

My mother Maxine was given the honour of ringing the church bell. The weekend was indescribably special and, as we visited the site of the Maopo home and took the pathway past the house to the ocean, we reflected that Phoebe and Wiremu would no doubt have taken many a walk down this pathway to the beach.

As my daughter and I stood on the shore, two dolphins jumped and dived in the waves before us, confirming that this was indeed a special time. The Taumutu whānau were hospitable and embracing beyond words and, when things couldn't possibly be better, they loaded us with packages of smoked eel fresh from the lake. Despite having eaten North Island eels for many years, none ever tasted as sweet.

With this linkage came our identity, our heritage, and a vast set of historical knowledge. Our whānau remains extremely grateful and indebted to all who helped to make the connection. Wiremu's descendants now number around 40 and we are expanding. As for our tūpuna, Wiremu and Phoebe, we will never forget.

Te ruru a te ihonga e kore e taea te māwete.
A kinship bond can never be untied.

Kua Mutu

18

Maopo whakapapa

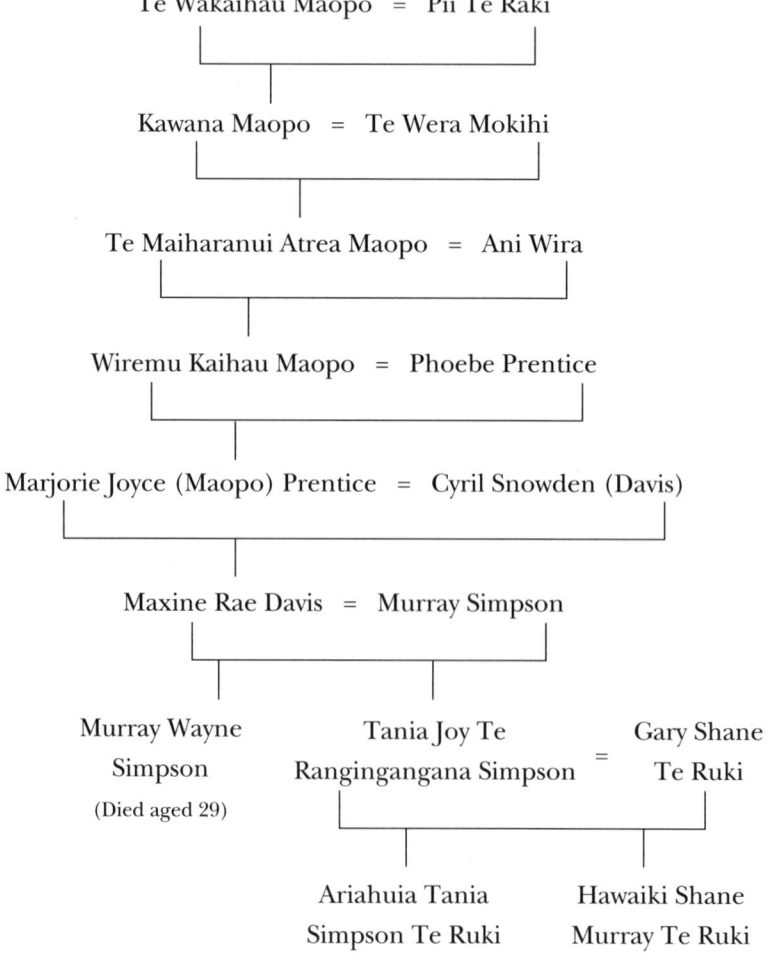

Acknowledgements

Kāore he mutunga o āku mihi ki a koutou e te hunga i tautoko mai, i āwhina mai hoki i ngā mahi rangahau. Ko koutou ngā ringa hāpai i te kaupapa ma te pō-kākaraui ki a te ao mārama. He mihi aroha, he mihi maioha ki a koutou e aku rangatira:

Rosaline Brown	Ellesmere Historical Society
Ron Crosby	Mary Johnston
Roger Gilbert	Peter Caldwell
Richard Manning	Virgie Mossop (née Fincham)
Brent Nunns	Graeme Nutira
Rose Nutira	Joan Overhill
Terry Ryan	Taumutu Rūnaka
Millie Schnelle	Denise Sheat
Shane Te Ruki	Malcolm Wards
Betty Welch	Peter Dowling
Niketi Toataua	Carolyn Lagahetau
Garth Cant	

Māori Soldiers Trust
Lottery World War One Commemorations, Environment and
    Heritage Committee
Maori Purposes Fund Board
The Ngāi Tahu Fund, Te Rūnanga o Ngāi Tahu

Author's note

I embarked on writing this story initially so that my children could know about their history and ancestry. It has been pieced together from research that I have undertaken over more than 20 years.

This research is not motivated by any intention or interest in claiming entitlements or benefits. The Maopo lands were given to Wiremu's adopted son and are now with the Manning family. Our family has no claim on these lands as a result of the history of our circumstance, and no one in our family should seek to claim any rights to these lands.

The only rights that we should be concerned with are the rights to know who we are and where we come from: our whakapapa, ancestry and the location of our traditional ancestral lands.

If anyone has any additional or contrary information to that which I have given in this story, please feel free to contact me. I am interested in portraying an accurate account so any further information is welcome. I especially apologise if I have anything wrong in relation to any of the people mentioned. The story is pieced together from fragments of information from people's memories and may not give a whole or accurate picture. It will no doubt continue to grow and develop as more information comes forward.

Tania Joy Te Rangingangana Simpson

Events in Wiremu's life

Pre-wartime events

1840	Treaty of Waitangi signed
1844	Tiakikai and Maopo are Taumutu rangatira
1845	Wesleyan missionary Charles Creed visits Taumutu
1848	Kawana Maopo signs Kemp's Purchase
1849	Surveyors in Taumutu stay with Kawana Maopo
1850s	Kawana Maopo has two wives, Wera Moki and Ngarara
1866	Kawana is an active leader at an estimated age of 78
1868	Kawana is a Trustee of the Native Reserve at Taumutu
1870s	Hone Kerei Taiaroa shifts from Otakou to Taumutu
1878	Awhitu House built at Taumutu for whānau of H.K. Taiaroa
1883	Sedgemere School opened: Māori and Pākehā children admitted
1885	Hone Wetere Church built and opened at Taumutu Pā
1886	Wiremu Maopo born
1889	Lease records for lands leased from Te Maiharanui Maopo
1898	Phoebe born
25 March 1909	Atarea Maopo elected as Taumutu representative for Māori Council
20 April 1913	Harry Maopo dies, age 24

1913	Harry Maopo's funeral; Harry was the tenth child of Te Maiharanui to die due to illness
	Ani Wera Maopo, Te Maiharanui's wife, also dies and is farewelled
1914	Taare Maopo dies, the eleventh child of Te Maiharanui to pass away due to illness
4 August 1914	First World War declared

1915

25 April	Gallipoli battle begins
29 June	Wiremu commences training
6 Jul–21 Aug	At Māori Camp, Fort Takapuna, Auckland
September	Phoebe discovers she is pregnant
18 September	Wiremu farewells Taumutu and friends
7 October	Departs New Zealand on troopship *Waitemata*
19 December	At Zeitoun Camp, Cairo, Egypt
20 December	Battle at Gallipoli ends

1916

28 January	Stationed at The Canal, Egypt
29 February	Stationed at Moascar Camp, Egypt
8 March	Phoebe gives birth to daughter Marjorie Joyce
17 March	Wiremu's birthday
22 March	Te Maiharanui Maopo dies
May	New Zealanders arrive in France
23–30 May	In France
18 July	Death of Mr Maopo acknowledged in the *Methodist Quarterly*
August	Hinewai gives birth to daughter, Edna Cant
November	Phoebe returns home with Marjorie Joyce, aged eight months; Marjorie Joyce is taken from her and placed in a forced adoption
9 Nov–25 Dec	In France

1917

28 Jan–9 Apr	In France
19 May–5 Jun	In Belgium
July	Fred and Emma Schnelle leave Taumutu to live in Oparure, Te Kuiti
6 July	In London on leave
20 July	In the field, including at Messines and Somme
1 August	In the field
14 August	Hinewai's baby, Edna, dies
16–26 Aug	In the field
31 October	In France, mentions fighting at Ypres
6 November	In France
14 November	In the field
28 November	Phoebe and new husband Bill have a son
12–31 Dec	In the field

1918

1 Jan–28 Feb	In the field
2 April	Wiremu ill with pneumonia
9 April	Wiremu reported as dangerously ill
18 April	Wiremu removed from dangerously ill list
23 April	Taumutu papers report that Wiremu is seriously ill
3 May	In London, Wiremu sick with pleuro-pneumonia
29 June	In London recovering from influenza Visits Scotland
11 September	*Ellesmere Guardian* reports that Wiremu will be home within next fortnight
24 September	Wiremu arrives at Lyttleton
2 October	Welcome home advert published
4 October	Attends a welcome home function
5 October	Welcome home function reported in local newspaper
22 November	Wiremu discharged from the army
28 December	Phoebe and husband Bill have a daughter, Madeleine Olive Bonsy (Bonny)

❦   The Last *Maopo*

23 June 1919   Presentation of medals at Taumutu

March 1926   Hinewai dies, aged 35

25 November 1927   Wiremu boarding with Charles Thomas

1928   Phoebe finds and reunites with her daughter, Marjorie Joyce

12 July 1929   Wiremu dies, aged 43

Notes

1 Reconnecting
1. The member of the rūnanga that made the connection was Malcolm Wards' mother.

2 The early Maopo whānau
1. http://christchurchcitylibraries.com/TiKoukaWhenua/Waihora
2. http://christchurchcitylibraries.com/TiKoukaWhenua/NgātiMoki
3. http://keteselwyn.peoplesnetworknz.info/places_of_interest/topics Taumutu
4. Magistrate Robinson's population return for 1843 (WArc: IA 1 44/607); Edward Shortland. Table showing the Amount of Native Population, enclosure with his report of 18 March 1844 (BPP NZ 51846 (337) 153-9). Cited in Antoine Edouard Foley's Eki (Paris: 1874). Thesis by Colin Kelly, University of Canterbury 2004.
5. http://christchurchcitylibraries.com/TiKoukaWhenua/Waihora
6. See Collins, 'Auguste Delatre, interprète de Charles Meryon', *Gazette des beaux-arts*, 1983, 173–74. Cited in Antoine Edouard Foley's Eki (Paris: 1874). Thesis by Colin Kelly, University of Canterbury 2004.
7. Kelly, op. cit., p. 81.
8. Information from Taumutu elder, Rosaline Brown.
9. Patterson, Murray (1929–98), *In Sight of the Lake & Sound of the Sea*. M. Patterson, Leeston, New Zealand, 1998.
10. ibid., p. 331.
11. ibid., p. 266.
12. ibid., p. 331.
13. Sedgemere School Centennial Roll, 1883–1983.
14. Patterson, op. cit., p. 266.

3 Wiremu Kaihau Maopo meets Phoebe Prentice
1. 'Our Women of the Past, Women of Sedgemere and Taumutu', Vol. 1. An article about Mary Fincham written by her great-granddaughter, Mary Hastings, 1933.
2. ibid.
3. Patterson, Murray (1929–98), *In Sight of the Lake & Sound of the Sea*. M. Patterson, Leeston, New Zealand, 1998, p. 252.

4. Letter from Garth Cant to the author, 31 January 2010.

4 Wiremu goes to war
1. Cowan, J., *The Maoris in the Great War: a history of the New Zealand native contingent and Pioneer Battalion: Gallipoli, 1915: France and Flanders, 1916–1918*. Whitcombe & Tombs [for] Maori Regimental Committee, Auckland, 1926, p. 26.
2. ibid., p. 16.
3. ibid., p. 32.
4. ibid., p. 43.
5. ibid., p. 52.
6. ibid.
7. ibid., p. 54.
8. Old Phillip is Herini Tawera, who came to Taumutu from the Hawke's Bay during the time of Te Kooti.
9. Cowan, op. cit., citing Captain Buck, p. 68.
10. ibid., p. 68.

5 Phoebe goes to the Bethany Home
1. Carkeek, Rihihana, *Home Little Maori Home —A Memoir of the Maori Contingent, 1914–1916*. Tōtika Publications, Wellington, 2003.
2. War Diaries of NZ (Maori) Pioneer Battalion, February 1916.
3. op. cit., March 1916.

6 Phoebe's baby
1. Cowan, J., *The Maoris in the Great War: a history of the New Zealand native contingent and Pioneer Battalion: Gallipoli, 1915: France and Flanders, 1916–1918*. Whitcombe & Tombs [for] Maori Regimental Committee, Auckland, 1926, p. 73.

2. ibid., p. 77.
3. ibid., p. 78.
4. ibid., p. 79.

7 A world at war
1. Cowan, J., *The Maoris in the Great War: a history of the New Zealand native contingent and Pioneer Battalion: Gallipoli, 1915: France and Flanders, 1916–1918*. Whitcombe & Tombs [for] Maori Regimental Committee, Auckland, 1926, p. 80.
2. ibid., pp. 81–87.

8 Phoebe: moving on
1. Cowan, J., *The Maoris in the Great War: a history of the New Zealand native contingent and Pioneer Battalion: Gallipoli, 1915: France and Flanders, 1916–1918*. Whitcombe & Tombs [for] Maori Regimental Committee, Auckland, 1926, p. 108.

10 Wiremu visits 'Blighty'
1. Pugsley, Christopher, *Te Hokowhitu a Tu, The Maori Pioneer Battalion in the First World War*. Reed, Auckland, 1995. Citing a letter from Lt Col. G.A. King dated 7 July 1917, p. 65.

11 Changes at home
1. Cowan, J., *The Maoris in the Great War: a history of the New Zealand native contingent and Pioneer Battalion: Gallipoli, 1915: France and Flanders, 1916–1918*. Whitcombe & Tombs [for] Maori Regimental Committee, Auckland, 1926, p. 119.
2. War Diaries of NZ (Maori) Pioneer Battalion, September 1917.

3. op. cit., October 1917.
4. Pugsley, Christopher, *Te Hokowhitu a Tu, The Maori Pioneer Battalion in the First World War*, Reed, 1995. Newspaper clipping, Lt Col. G.A. King, letters and diaries, p. 67.
5. War Diary of NZ Maori (Pioneer) Battalion, November 1917.
6. ibid.

12 The onset of winter
1. War Diary of NZ (Maori) Pioneer Battalion, November 1917.
2. Pugsley, Christopher, *Te Hokowhitu a Tu, The Maori Pioneer Battalion in the First World War*, Reed, Auckland, 1995. Citing Reta a Henare Wainohu ki te Pihopa, 12 October 1917, p. 70, originally published in *Kahiti*, p. 10.
3. ibid.
4. Pugsley, op. cit., Headquarters New Zealand Division Instruction, 14 September 1917, WA 97/3/8, National Archives of New Zealand.
5. Pugsley, op cit., p. 67.
6. War Diary of the NZ (Maori) Pioneer Battalion, December 1917.
7. Cowan, J., *The Maoris in the Great War: a history of the New Zealand native contingent and Pioneer Battalion: Gallipoli, 1915: France and Flanders, 1916–1918.* Whitcombe & Tombs [for] Maori Regimental Committee, Auckland, 1926, p. 129.
8. War Diary of NZ (Maori) Pioneer Battalion, February 1918.
9. Pugsley, op. cit., p. 71.
10. Cowan, op. cit., p. 135.
11. War Diary of NZ (Maori) Pioneer Battalion, March 1918.

14 Wiremu returns home
1. Cowan, J., *The Maoris in the Great War: a history of the New Zealand native contingent and Pioneer Battalion: Gallipoli, 1915: France and Flanders, 1916–1918.* Whitcombe & Tombs [for] Maori Regimental Committee, Auckland, 1926. Citing Anzac Day address given by Hon. Sir Maui Pomare in 1926.

15 Life after war
1. Māori Land Court South Island Minute Book, No. 25, p. 251.
2. Information provided by Malcolm Wards.